R,I L TURNBULL 1969

Scope. Yes
0191 2840610

Cancer Re. Yes.
0191 2130009

Oxfam Yes
0191 2848991.

Mind Saltees lane.
2851808

2468123

The Pigeon
in the Wider World

Chinese pictogram, representing 'Pigeon', drawn by Sonia Lim

The Pigeon
in the
Wider World

Jean Hansell

Millstream Books

Acknowledgments

Following the publication of my earlier books (*see page 8 for details*) it became evident that the pigeon also played a role in religion and culture far beyond the confines of the Western World. In this attempt to expand the story in the wider world I have received help from many people including family and friends and this must be acknowledged, especially James Hansell for his photographic skills.

As before I am indebted to the late Barbara Frears, friend and architect, whose drawings and watercolours have greatly enlivened this, the fifth book to which she has contributed. I am also grateful to Brian McElney, OBE, of the Museum of East Asian Art in Bath for helpful advice about China, and to Professor David Goode on the same score.

Above all, my thanks go to Guy Merchant, friend and fellow pigeon-lover, who not only gave me immeasurable encouragement in the initial stages but later provided unfailing practical help with transcribing the original manuscripts.

My appreciation, as always to my publisher, Tim Graham of Millstream Books, who has taken on this fifth book in the series about the bird. He has been a pleasure to work with and a support at all times, and has maintained his usual high standard of production.

Illustrations in the book have been credited appropriately where possible. To the owners of material which I have been unable to acknowledge correctly, I beg indulgence.

First published in 2010 by Millstream Books, 18 The Tyning, Bath BA2 6AL

Set in Palatino and printed in Great Britain by The Short Run Press, Exeter

ISBN: 978 0 948975 91 2

Contents

Cover illustrations

*front: White doves on the roof of the Blue Mosque at Mazar-i-Sharif, Afghanistan.
        (Photograph by Babak Fakhamzadeh)*
rear: Detail from a Chinese incised lacquer screen, dated 1674. (Private collection)

Prologue

It all started after my husband had retired when we discovered dovecotes. Several years later, after we had written two books about these buildings, it was a short step to my becoming interested in the birds themselves. My two later books revealed how very useful the pigeon had been over the centuries in so many different parts of the world and also its special position in so many different societies. Nowadays, by contrast, it is dismaying to discover that among the general population the bird evokes such dislike. In many cities of the world, where most pigeons now live, they are often regarded as pests and a civic nuisance, the 'flying rats' of the popular press. Sadly, this overlooks their unusual character and most interesting history.

It is seldom recognised that these feral birds are the same as the white dove which returned with an olive leaf to Noah in the Ark at the end of the Deluge and which has become the enduring symbol of peace, reconciliation and goodwill still familiar today. Recently there have been attempts in Britain to reconcile the four great religions of the world, namely Christianity, Judaism, Islam and Buddhism, on the basis of origin and shared ideas. Perhaps the dove as a common symbol might have a claim to be included in such a plan.

The story of the bird has been much obscured by the age-long confusion between the names 'pigeon' and 'dove', both of which refer to the same bird, the Blue Rock Pigeon (*Columba livia*), and are still used interchangeably today, as I do in this book. In general, 'dove' is traditionally reserved for the aesthetic contexts of religion, literature and art, while 'pigeon' applies to matters such as sport, fancy birds and culinary use, although the French have a recipe for 'roast dove'.

There does not seem to be an obvious resemblance between the white dove of peace and the pigeon in a pie but they are both descended from the same pigeon which is found widely distributed except at the polar ice-caps. The bird's natural home is in the rocky ledges and niches of coastal and inland cliffs but it has an inborn affinity with man and a tendency to nest in and around his dwellings to the extent that man may have done no more than meet its advances half-way.

Having recently celebrated the bi-centenary year of the birth of Charles Darwin, it is appropriate to mention his work in establishing for the first time that the origin of all the many varieties of fancy pigeon was from the common Rock Pigeon. He added this as a microcosm of his theory of selective breeding in natural selection.

In many parts of the world, fragmentary evidence from earliest times has revealed how closely enmeshed the pigeon has become in different nations and cultures. Ranging from early paganism to monotheistic and other early beliefs, down through the centuries to the consumerism of the present day, the symbol of the dove still endures. No other bird has had such close links with man nor been useful to him in so many ways. It has served him as symbol, sacrifice, source of food and not least as a messenger in peace and war.

Early examples include its use in Sumeria as a symbol of the Great Mother Goddess; as a sacrificial offering, in both the Old and New Testaments as well as in the Classical era when it was sacrificed to the goddess Aphrodite (Venus); in domestication, when the young birds or squabs were bred in dovecotes in early Sumerian, Egyptian and Classical times; and finally as a messenger in peace and war which usage was widespread in many cultures not only in the West but also in the Muslim world, India, the Near East and China.

Among the pigeon's various attributes its role as messenger must count as the most outstanding, particularly its recent record in both World Wars. This is a little known epic, but even today stories of the bird's bravery and endurance, which resulted in many human lives being saved in the various services, still have the power to move. Man's debt to the pigeon's heroism has been recognised by civic memorials and individual awards, but no doubt very many birds died unknown and unrecorded.

The pigeon also played a minor role as bait and decoy in the early days of falconry and was massacred in large numbers in the shooting matches of later days. Even today the shooting of captive pigeons is still pursued as a sport in Pennsylvania. However, it was also popular in the more peaceful sport of *triganieri* which has ancient roots and was mentioned in the Jewish Talmud and recognised in the Classical world. This sport, which exploits the pigeons' tendency to fly together in flocks in the sky and with training to entice other competing birds back to their own loft, had an enthusiastic following in Persia, Egypt, Turkey, the Muslim world and parts of Europe, and is still followed today in various parts of the world The later sport of pigeon racing has a large following all over the world, Saudi Arabia and China providing the latest enthusiasts.

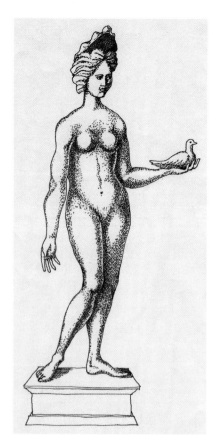

(left) An early Greek sculpture of a nude Aphrodite holding a dove in her hand. (Barbara Frears)
(right) A 21st-century version of a similar pose from Korean Air.

Nowadays the claim by experts that perception of the bird is changing for the better, together with a recent account in the press that pigeons are 'the tamest wild animals in the world, the most comfortable with human routines', is welcome but there is still some way to go.

As an octogenarian this will be my last contribution to the story of the bird that I have studied and written about for the past several decades. It supplements my previous books which focus largely on the Western World and is intended to expand the remarkable story of the pigeon in the wider world.

Further Reading

Hansell, Peter and Jean (1988), *Doves and Dovecotes*, Millstream Books, Bath
Hansell, Peter and Jean (1992), *A Dovecote Heritage*, Millstream Books, Bath
Hansell, Jean (1998), *The Pigeon in History*, Millstream Books, Bath
Hansell, Jean (2003), *Images of the Dove*, Millstream Books, Bath

The Early History of the Pigeon in the Near East

The ancient civilisation of Sumeria in south-west Asia, which flourished between c.5300 BC and c.1700 BC, contains the earliest references to the pigeon in the Near East. This region lies within the so-called Fertile Crescent of Mesopotamia at the head of the Persian Gulf and is bordered by ancient Babylonia and Assyria in the west and by Akkad and Elam (roughly corresponding to Iran) in the east. It was here that early hunter-gatherers developed the cultivation of crops, as early as 10,000 BC. This was eventually followed by the domestication of animals such as dogs, goats, pigs, sheep and cattle between 8000 BC and 6000 BC. Although recent writers on the subject have not included the pigeon specifically among these, it seems reasonable to assume that grain-farmers on the banks of the Tigris and Euphrates would have been quick to tame the bird. It has been claimed that the pigeon was the first of all the birds to be domesticated and the Sumerians are thought to have been among the first in the region to breed birds from the indigenous Blue Rock Pigeon. Not only does the bird have an inborn affinity with man but the value of its meat, eggs and feathers would have been very useful to him. The situation would no doubt have been comparable in ancient Egypt on the banks of the Nile.

One of the most momentous contributions of the Sumerians, c.3500 BC, was the art of writing. The discovery of thousands of clay tablets excavated from the city of Uruk in Sumeria revealed the earliest of all texts inscribed in a complex mixture which came to be known as cuneiform. Much of this has now been deciphered to reveal an extensive literature comprising hymns and poems together with proverbs and mythical and epic tales.

Bronze figure of a goddess surmounted by a dove from the second millennium BC. (Metropolitan Museum of Art, Chapman Fund, 1966)

9

Scattered allusions to pigeons are found in these tablets including references to the birds' role as temple birds of the goddess. At a time when strife existed between Northern and Southern Sumerians we read 'the temple window was destroyed, its doves flew away'. Also revealing are the words recorded by one of the many goddesses linked with the bird: 'the dovecotes they wickedly seized, the doves they entrapped', while another goddess who identifies herself with the bird bemoans in a psalm: 'like a dove to its dwelling place, how long to my dwelling place will they pursue me?' Finally, from a recently translated Sumerian text:

> you go to the house of the bird catcher and you buy two doves, male and female. You return to your house. The courtyard of the house, you fumigate, you sprinkle with water ... you set up a portable altar ... you release the fetters of the two doves ... then you let the male dove fly to the east and the female dove fly to the west.

Initially this suggests that a sacrifice might be intended; however, this bird-release ritual is mentioned elsewhere. Its exact purpose seems to be obscure although it might be a substitute for a sacrificial offering. A modern writer comments that the Sumerians did not use imaginary descriptions but based their imagery on stern facts which often carried a religious significance; in this case not only the relation between goddess, temple and dove but also the surprisingly early existence of dovecotes.

The Epic of Gilgamesh, written in about 2000 BC and preserved on twelve tablets, centres around the supreme hero of Sumerian myth and legends and the historical King of Uruk, and also includes an early story of the Deluge. It relates the story of the goddess who intended to save humanity from the flood; the raven and the dove, together with the swallow, were sent out to test the abatement of the waters. It has been postulated that the pigeon and raven might originally have been sacred totems among primitive local tribes.

(left) A dove, supposedly a sacrifice, being offered to a goddess, on a Persian cylinder seal of the 3rd to 7th centuries AD. (Barbara Frears)

(right) Relief of an enthroned Sumerian goddess with sacred trees and birds, probably doves.

10

(left) Votive dove in lapis-lazuli with gold studs from the Acropolis of Susa. (The Louvre, Paris)
(right) A pair of billing doves in stone from Mesopotamia, 2900-2800 BC. (Irit Ziffer)

The recent archaeological discovery at Uruk in southern Sumeria of early remains of temples dating from 5000-4900 BC together with other later finds of female figurines beside life-like terracotta models of pigeons, assumed to be votive offerings, have provided an early link between the goddess and the bird. Many of the finds are damaged but at Tall Arpachiyah (in today's Iraq) painted eyes and feathers can still be seen on one of the birds.

It has been suggested that the pigeon's natural affinity with man allied to its tendency to nest in his dwellings would have encouraged its domestication when protected in temples of early goddesses. The discovery at Al'Ubaid in southern Sumeria of remains of the temple dedicated to the goddess Ninhursag, dating from 3000 BC, provides one piece of evidence for this conjecture. On the reconstructed outer façade (*shown below and on the next page*), a limestone frieze depicting cows of the temple herd being milked is matched by another showing a row of sitting pigeons. In

Part of the façade of the temple of Ninhursag showing a row of sitting pigeons. (British Museum, photograph by Peter Hansell)

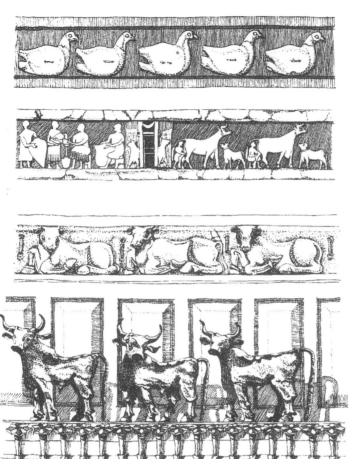

ancient times domesticated herds and flocks, together with their produce, were under the protection of the goddess. In her primitive sacred enclosures, cows and sheep were housed and later, together with the granary and possibly the pigeon-house, they would have occupied the temple precincts. As in Egypt she was sometimes portrayed as the great cow offering milk to her people.

In southern Sumeria, Ninhursag's role was perpetuated and later eclipsed by Inanna, goddess of the Great Above and the Great Below, whose name was derived from Iahu, Ia meaning the exalted one or moon-goddess in the form of a cow and Hu, the same goddess in dove form. The semitic Akkadians in northern Sumeria called her Ishtar who also had a dove form. Both goddesses were worshipped as Queen of Heaven, their principal other images being the moon, the planet Venus, and the morning and evening stars.

A bronze decoration known as the dove-goddess, possibly linked with Ishtar. (Barbara Frears)

12

A further version was Anahita, recognised in Sumeria and Babylonia and later adopted into the religion of Zoroastrianism which dates from 600 BC. She was known as the goddess of water and of animal and human fertility, also as the Golden Mother and Warrior Maiden. It has been recorded that ritual prostitution took place in her temples 'to purify the seed of the males and the womb and milk of the females'; she was honoured with green branches and received the sacrifice of white heifers. Her symbols were the dove and the peacock.

A curious link which traces trees and gender as cultural symbols of the goddesses has recently been established between them and the fruiting date-palm tree. Several cylinder seals reveal the association and include not only the tree but branches of its clusters being gathered by women. It is said that the feminine association encompasses both the divine and the mortal worlds. One intriguing example is an ivory box from Assur (*shown below*), intended to contain holy objects, which is incised with a frieze showing a row of conifer trees alternating with fruiting date-palms. A pair of birds is perched on the top of each tree, cocks on the conifers while those on the date-palms are described as hens, which might seem an obvious explanation, but they could be identified as pigeons owing to their association with the goddess, particularly her role in fecundity. The cones of the conifer trees are symbols of the male gods.

(above) A later version of the goddess Anahita, holding a dove in her hand, beneath an arch decorated with pigeons. (Barbara Frears)

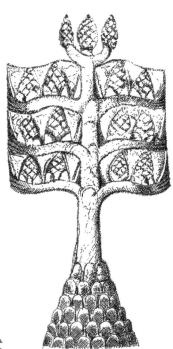

(above) Symbolic representation of cone-bearing conifers.

Although the Great Goddess was the supreme deity in Sumeria as in most other primitive societies, the existence of a son-brother-consort added to the pantheon. Known by several names including the Green One, the Fish God and Lord of the Sheepfold and Cattle Byre, some of these titles seem to have been transferred from the goddess herself; similarly another description of him as 'he of the dovecote voice, yea dovelike!' Enki, son-lover of Ninhursag who became one of the great gods of Sumeria, is shown on a cylinder seal with his symbols, a fish within a stream of water representing the divine fluid, a

The god Enki with his symbols, as shown on a cylinder seal.

bird in his hand, probably a dove, and a small sitting creature, possibly a lamb.

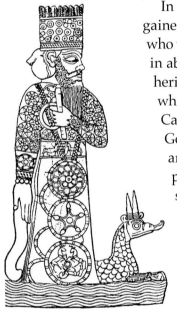

The god Marduk with his dragon, from a lapi-lazuli cylinder of the 9th century BC.

In the early days of Sumeria the northern Akkadians gained control over the indigenous people of the south who were later conquered by the Babylonians to the west in about 1900 BC. They were thus a mixed race who inherited the literature, mythology and laws of Sumeria which later spread throughout Assyria, Anatolia, Canaan and beyond. Ishtar, the Babylonian Great Goddess, was sometimes depicted in bird form but in answer to the ravages of war greater emphasis was placed on her martial aspects. This was related in several legends concerning the god Marduk which tells of the rise to dominance of the Father God, while the goddess became known as the Serpent Goddess. The Hebrew prophets knew the goddess as the Moon or Sea-goddess but regarded her as the mistress of all fleshy corruptions.

Many terracotta shrines of the goddess have been excavated in Assyria. A rectangular roofless model from Assur, possibly a Sumerian survival, is dominated by a large sheep on the parapet with figures of pigeons in the wall below. One shrine excavated from the site of the temple of Ishtar may date from about 2000 BC. It features symbolic doves and snakes of the goddess, the former in rows and the latter coiling around the walls. The serpent was an extremely ancient link with the goddess. In the city of Uruk two very early images of the goddess and her child have been found both of whom have the heads of serpents.

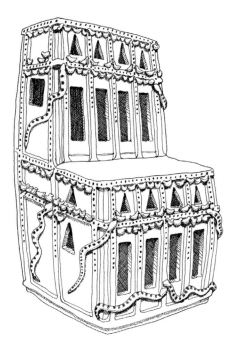

(left) Terracotta shrine from Assur, 2400-2200 BC.
(right) Clay model from the temple of Ishtar in Asur with dove and snake motifs. (Barbara Frears)

An archaic legend of both Babylonia and Assyria describes the birth of the goddess from an immense egg which fell from heaven into the Euphrates where it was rolled ashore by a fish and hatched by doves. It neatly incorporates the ancient symbols of egg, bird and fish. Another myth of great antiquity tells of the Fish-goddess Derceto who abandoned her new-born baby which was adopted by shepherds and nourished by doves. She grew up to become Semiramis ('the Dove goddess loves her child'); at the end of her life she changed herself into a dove and flew away. Another variation relates that she was transformed into the bird Inyx and was crucified on a wheel with four spokes. In these and other versions she was worshipped thereafter as a glorious mystery and is reputed to have been the founder of the city of Babylon.

(left) A medal showing Semiramis holding her dove and standing on fish-tailed Derceto.

(right) Semiramis transformed into the bird Inyx and sacrificed on a wheel.

15

The scene of a bas-relief from Nimroud, Assyria, entitled 'Idols and Captives from a Conquered Nation' depicts the large figure of a dove being carried aloft on a platform by victorious warriors while captives linger alongside. It has been surmised that this represents the practice among the ancients of removing or destroying images of deities belonging to the vanquished. In Assyria this might have taken place at a time when there was a resurgence of Mother Goddess worship among those of Sumerian or Akkadian descent.

Idols and captives from a bas-relief of Nimroud showing a pigeon being carried aloft on a platform. (Barbara Frears)

The fragmentary evidence on the pigeon in this region chiefly emphasises its position as a symbol and possible sacrifice to the Great Mother Goddess. By contrast, however, there is later evidence of its use as as a messenger bird, particularly in the Arab world. A large-scale system of communication using pigeons had been established in the 5th century BC in Assyria and much later in Baghdad which was linked with Egypt and other cities in the eastern Mediterranean.

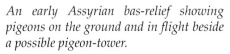

An early Assyrian bas-relief showing pigeons on the ground and in flight beside a possible pigeon-tower.

The Carrier cock, painted by J.W. Ludlow, from Robert Fulton's Illustrated Book of Pigeons, 1895.

It is a curious fact that although the bird was fleetingly alluded to in earliest times in Sumeria very little is recorded about its habitation until much later. In the 17th century an English traveller who visited Isfahan wrote: 'I don't think there are finer Dove-cotes in any part of the world'. He estimated that there were more than 3,000 pigeon-towers within 31 miles of that city, used to produce guano for the production of melons. At that period the right to build a dovecote was restricted to Muslims, and a French visitor caustically records that some Christians adopted the Muslim faith in order to gain the privilege.

Scene of a dovecote and pigeon-keeper with various birds, from an 18th-century Arab treatise. (The British Library, Ms IO Persian 4811, fol.5)

The region is also important in being the origin of the well-known Wattle pigeons, known in the West as the Baghdad or Eastern Carrier, and ancestor of today's racing homers. Later, particularly in the West, Persia had a reputation as the home of expert pigeon fanciers. It has been suggested that the exchange of special fancy birds took place by way of ancient trade routes such as the Silk Road, which connected the Mediterranean with the Orient. The sport of *triganieri* was popular in ancient Persia and continues today. The fortunate survival of an illustrated 18th-century Arab treatise, describing various aspects of pigeon-keeping, also includes scenes of the birds and their keepers.

Further north, in present-day western Afghanistan, near the Iran border, large decorated dovecotes, believed to have been built in the 17th century, were located around the city of Herat. This town lies on what was once the old trade route from Persia to India and on the caravan trail from China to Central Asia. The present state of the pigeon-towers in Iran and Afghanistan is not known although it seems likely that conflicts in the region will have resulted in their damage or loss.

(above) A 17th-century decorated pigeon-house in Isfahan.
(below) Decorated pigeon-towers in Western Afghanistan, depicted around a century ago.

An example of a large pigeon-tower from Iran.
Note the size of the human figure standing at the front.
(Dr. G.C.L. Bertram)

Further Reading

Baring, Anne & Cashford, Jules (1993), *The Myth of the Goddess*, Penguin Books, Harmondsworth

Houghton, William (1884), 'The Birds of the Assyrian Monuments and Records',
    Transactions of the Society of Biblical Archaeology, Vol.VII, Part 1, London

James, E.O. (1951), *The Cult of the Mother Goddess*, Thames & Hudson, London

Lucian (1913), *The Syrian Goddess* (translation of *De Dea Syria* by W.H. Strong),
    Constable, London

MacKenzie, D.A. (1915), *Myths of Babylonia and Assyria*, Gresham Publishing Company, London

Neumann, E. (1955), *The Great Mother: An Analysis of the Archetype*, Routledge & Kegan
    Paul, London

Sayce, A.H. (1900), *Babylonians and Assyrians: Life and Customs*, Routledge & Kegan Paul, London

Woolley, C.L. (1927), *The Sumerians*, Oxford University Press, Oxford

Zaehner, R.C. (1961), *The Dawn and Twilight of Zoroastrianism*, Weidenfeld & Nicolson, London

Zeuner, Frederick E. (1963), *A History of Domesticated Animals*, Hutchinson, London

Ziffer, I. (1998), *O my dove that art in the cleft of the rocks: The Dove-allegory in Antiquity*, Eretz
    Israel Museum, Tel Aviv

The Pigeon in Egypt

It is probable that the pigeon was familiar in Egypt since earliest times although actual traces and records of the birds are few and far between. The well-preserved pottery model from the Gerzean period (3500-3200 BC) is a rare example while a contrasting figure in glass dates from 1000-700 BC.

Early Egyptian pottery model of a pigeon, 3500-3200 BC.

Egyptian figure of a dove in dark brown glass, 1000-700 BC. (Irit Ziffer)

Unlike neighbouring Sumeria where the dove was a sacred symbol of the Great Mother Goddess, it does not appear to have been a divine image among the large pantheon of Egyptian deities. In the case of the goddess Isis, for example, wife of the god Osiris and once described as being 'receptive of all manner of shapes and forms', many creatures have been linked with her but the pigeon is an exception. Apart from this, however, Charles Sibillot, writing a century or so ago, claimed that the bird he named the Messenger of Osiris should be included. This breed of ancient origin was characterised by having a curved beak and belongs to the group of Eastern Carriers which includes the Scandaroon pigeon. Another bird, known as the Starling or Moon-bird which has a crescent-shaped mark on the breast, was named by him as the Dove of Isis. Away from the realms of

The Starling, Sibillot's 'Dove of Isis', painted by J.W. Ludlow, from Robert Fulton's Illustrated Book of Pigeons, 1895.

the gods he finally claimed that the Swift variety of pigeon was known as the favourite and messenger of the ancient Rameses Kings of Egypt.

From earliest times the so-called 'pigeon mail' connected Egypt and the Near East. In ancient Egypt, the birds played an important role in sending news of the progress of the river in the annual flooding of the Nile which was of such vital importance to the fertility of the land. Sibillot described the way in which pigeons carried the news in the past by means of a relay of 'pigeon-posts' along the length of the river. At these points, the priests of Osiris, one of whose titles was God of the fertility of the Nile, awaited the arrival of the birds which had been released in the upper reaches and whose appearance preceded the river's surge. Once they had returned, general rejoicing ensued to celebrate the return of fertility, the God himself being said to have symbolically arrived.

In Egypt, as in many other cultures of the Near East, birds were worshipped as spiritual links between heaven and earth. In the past they were believed to accompany the soul to heaven and later to return as the Spirit of the Departed to its last resting place. Symbolically they were depicted in different ways, often as the winged sun-disk and pigeon linked with the Egyptian god Aten. An early relief from Canaan dating from 1200 BC shows a goddess surmounted by the symbol and holding a dove in each hand. In Egyptian art its counterpart was the soul-bird which sometimes had the head of a falcon, symbol of the god Horus, son of Osiris and Isis, and in a few cases it was given a human head. Centuries later, literary evidence confirms the endurance of this belief in the dove as a soul-bird in the writings of St Ambrose: 'That soul is blessed, simple in every respect. That soul accordingly is a dove'.

(left) Relief of a goddess holding a dove in each hand, with a sun-disk above. (Barbara Frears)
(right) A winged Egyptian soul-bird visiting a corpse, carrying the ankh, symbol of life.

In ancient Egypt an intriguing link with Christianity is to be found in the monastery of St Anthony on the Red Sea founded by the Coptic orthodox church in the 12th-13th centuries or possibly earlier. Conservation which started in the last two decades has revealed remarkable wall paintings in the Coptic artistic tradition. In one chapel of the sanctuary the so-called four living creatures, as described in the Book of Revelation in the New Testament, are depicted guarding the grand throne of Christ in Majesty. They have four wings and their bodies are covered with eyes but the most singular feature is that among the character-istic heads of lion, calf, face of man and eagle, the latter is replaced by the un-mistakable head of a pigeon (*shown right*).

Another early Egyptian symbol, the Uroborus, was depicted as a serpent with its tail in its mouth which symbolised eternity and was linked with the underworld. Later it was adopted into Christianity and occasionally depicted with a central dove when it was believed additionally to represent the Comforter (the Holy Spirit), as well as healing and deliverance.

(left) The Uroborus and dove motif.

Although the evidence is sketchy the pigeon appears to have been a favourite table food in Egypt. The birds are depicted in decorative reliefs and wall-paintings, often together with ducks and geese; sometimes the pigeons appear on tombs where they are being carried, either dead or alive, as food for the deceased. A puzzling epithet in the annals of Rameses III (1182-1151 BC) includes his donation to a temple: 'I made to thee stables containing young oxen, an apartment to bring up fowls' (pigeons or birds of heaven). A further record states that Rameses offered 57,810 pigeons to the god Ammon at Thebes. It is not clear whether these birds would have been bred in the farmyard or whether domestication and the construction of dovecotes had been established but an early tomb painting from Thebes suggests that this was already the case. There seems little doubt that pigeon-rearing was an essential activity, not only to provide squabs but also for valuable manure. Excavations at Karanis, south of Cairo, have revealed the remains of domestic buildings of the later Roman occupation dating from about 30 BC. In the case of one courtyard, a roofless ruined dovecote was found which contained remains of nest boxes made from earthenware clay pots.

(right) The transport of fowl, possibly pigeons, by hand and in a cage, from a tomb at Saqqara, c.2250 BC.

(right) Depiction of an early tomb painting of a pigeon-house with birds. (Sara Roadnight)

(below) Force-feeding a pigeon, from a bas-relief, c.2500 BC. (Sara Roadnight)

Today pigeons are reared for food on a large scale in specially constructed dovecote towers sometimes housing many thousands of birds. By contrast, a smaller version has recently come to light in a modern Egyptian tapestry entitled 'Pigeon Tower in the Village' which was recently exhibited at the 'Nature in Art' museum in Gloucestershire. The example shown on the next pages comes from the Ramses Wissa Wassef Arts Centre in Cairo, founded in 1951 with the aim of releasing the innate creativity of young Egyptian villagers. To this end the founder established an after-school club in which the craft of high-warp weaving was taught and this tradition continues at the present day. The tapestry vividly portrays aspects of busy village life including the pigeon-tower with the birds alighting and in flight while others are being fed with grain on the ground.

Modern tapestry from the Ramses Wissa Wassef Arts Centre in Cairo, showing pigeons and a dovec

(left) Detail from a Roman mosaic dating from 200 BC showing a priest emerging from a shrine beside a dovecote with several pigeons in flight above the roof. (Museo Archeologico Nazionale di Palestrina, photograph by Paul Hansell)

(left) A present-day dovecote at Fayoum, with beehives in front. (Dr. W.F. Hollander)

(below) Present-day pigeon-towers on the Nile delta, with enlarged detail on the right.

It is believed that a pigeon post connected Egypt with the main cities of Alexandria, Jerusalem, Damascus and Baghdad at an early date. It is known that in 1160 AD the Fatimid Caliphs of Cairo had established a carrier pigeon service using the Baghdad Carrier and the Syrian Dewlap breeds. The service was well-organised with manned stopping places or lofts on the way and sometimes helped by post-horses in between. As the birds only fly in one direction each loft had a drove of mules or camels to return them to their home loft. It has been conjectured that the bas-relief showing the release of four pigeons during the coronation of Rameses II, c.1260 BC, is the earliest representation of the custom. It is believed that each bird is being released to announce the coronation of the King to the four points of the earth, but the exact explanation is disputed.

(left) The Syrian Dewlap

(above) Release of four pigeons during the coronation of Rameses II.

Fables of the past, sometimes defined as tales with moral and other abstract meanings have ancient classical roots and were common in countries such as Egypt, Africa and India in which animal worship once prevailed. An example in the 5th century, written by the Egyptian Horapollo, links the lives of animals and man allegorically. The pigeon is included in several rather unexpected ways. As a black dove it is said to denote a woman who remains a widow until death, 'for this bird has no connexion with another mate from the time that it is widowed', not a very accurate observation in practice.

(right) Fable of the black dove. (Barbara Frears)

In another example a dove is claimed to represent 'a man that is ungrateful and quarrelsome with his benefactors because when the male bird becomes stronger he drives the cock away from the hen and mates himself with her'. Almost as an afterthought a piece of dietary advice is given about the bird:

> *the creature seems to be pure, however, because when any pestilential epidemic rages and everything animate and inanimate sickens with disease those persons who alone feed upon this bird do not share so great a calamity – Wherefore during such a time nothing is served up to the King as food except the dove alone.*

The Book of the Dead is a name given to a collection of papyrus sheets covered with magical texts and illustrations which the Egyptians placed with their dead to help them pass through the dangers of the underworld and thus to attain an after-life of bliss in the Egyptian heaven. Among the many spells the pigeon is briefly mentioned:

> *May the pigeons waken you when you are asleep ... You are Horus son of Hathor, the male and female fiery serpents to whom was given a head after it had been cut off. Your head shall not be taken from you afterwards, your head shall not be taken from you for ever.*

These mysterious allusions are difficult to interpret but are included here to illustrate that the pigeon was enmeshed with many traditions of early Egyptian life.

Among other strange customs concerning death-rituals was the plaster mask made after the corpse had been mummified; it would have originally been painted and gilded. The example shown came together with others from Graeco-Egyptian cemeteries probably dating from the second century AD. It represents the bust of a boy called Herakleon and shows him holding a bunch of grapes in one hand and in the other a bird described as having a red beak and legs, the body being coloured blue with black markings, probably a dove. This is an unusual association as pigeons do not eat grapes, although occasionally it appears elsewhere, as for example on an early sarcophagus in southern France.

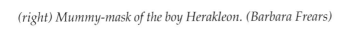

(right) Mummy-mask of the boy Herakleon. (Barbara Frears)

28

Although pigeons were used as messengers in the past there is little evidence of pigeon racing until more recently. By contrast, however, in Egypt today the competition of High-Flying Swifts, a variation of *triganieri*, is considered to be among the most exciting and challenging of sports. It has been claimed recently that for every racing pigeon follower in the country there are approximately 20 who keep birds for the competition of High Flying.

An Egyptian roof-top loft.

Contests generally take place on a friendly basis but can sometimes be fiercely competitive. An account by an American sea captain on a visit to Cairo in 1922 was recorded by E. Dietz and gives a vivid description of the sport in action from a roof-top loft. Rows of pens were arranged in a square with a place for the owner in one corner. The pigeons, largely Swifts and Oriental Rollers, were released at a signal, simultaneously with those from nearby lofts, and were then allowed to fly together before being recalled at another signal. On the occasion described the score was one bird lost and eleven captured, all of which were killed at once, one foot from each bird being cut off and hung up as a trophy on the wooden door.

The Swift is an interesting breed of pigeon, so-called because of its resemblance to the more familiar avian species, the swallow and swift. It is descended from earlier Carrier stock but was not mentioned by early European writers and only introduced into Britain in the 19th century. In appearance it has a large wing-span and a wedge-shaped tail; it resembles a hawk in flight and has great powers of endurance.

The Swift, painted by J.W. Ludlow, from Robert Fulton's Illustrated Book of Pigeons, 1895.

Today there are many pigeon fanciers who breed Egyptian Swifts and Rollers, both in Egypt and in many other parts of the world. The birds are classified in different variations of colour including bi-coloured and multi-coloured. The unusual hawk-like Scandaroon bird with its markedly curved beak is also of ancient origin and is raised by fanciers in the UK, Europe and the USA.

Oriental Rollers, drawn by J.W. Ludlow,
from Robert Fulton's Illustrated Book of Pigeons, 1895.

Further Reading

Budge, E.A. Wallis (1904), *The Gods of the Egyptians*, Methuen, London

Darby, William; Ghalioungui, Paul & Grivetti, Louis (1977), *Food: the Gift of Osiris*, Academic Press, London & New York

Davies, J.T. (1910), *The Burden of Isis*, John Murray, London

Emery, W.B. (1962), *Ancient Egypt*, Penguin Books, Harmondsworth

Faulkner, R.O. (1972), *The Ancient Egyptian Book of the Dead*, University of Texas Press, Austin (Tx.)

Fulton, Robert (1895), *The Illustrated Book of Pigeons*, Cassell, London

Glanville, S.R.K. (1942), *The Legacy of Egypt*, Clarendon Press, Oxford

Ions, Veronica (1968), *Egyptian Mythology*, Hamlyn, London

James, T.G.H. (1969), *Myths and Legends of Ancient Egypt*, Hamlyn, London

James, T.G.H. (1979), *An Introduction to Ancient Egypt* (based on *General Introductory Guide to the Egyptian Collections in the British Museum*, 1964), British Museum Press, London

Lurker, M. (1974), *The Gods and Symbols of Ancient Egypt*, Thames and Hudson, London & New York

Maspero, G. (1910), *The Struggle of the Nations: Egypt, Syria and Assyria*, S.P.C.K., London

Massey, Gerald (1907), *Ancient Egypt, the Light of the World*, T. Fisher Unwin, London

Parsons, P.J. (2007), *The City of the Sharp-nosed Fish*, Weidenfeld & Nicolson, London

Petrie, W.M. Flinders (1906), *The Religion of Ancient Egypt*, Constable, London

Roberts, M.D.L. & Gale, V.E. (2000), *Pigeons, Doves and Dovecotes*, Gold Cockerel Books, Crediton

Sibillot, C. (1916) *Lo Sport Colombofilo negli antichi tempi*, trans. R. Sacerdoti, Modena

Tarn, W.W. (1948), *Alexnder the Great*, Cambridge University Press, Cambridge

Wilkinson, J. Gardner (1878), *The Manners and Customs of the Ancient Egyptians*, John Murray, London

The Pigeon in Early Greece and Italy

In the classical world of Greece and Rome, a reference is found in the Homeric epic *The Iliad*, composed around the 9th century BC, to 'Messe's towers for silver doves renowned' which suggests that the pigeon was familiar in Greece at an early date. Another literary trace of the bird is found in the 6th-century BC poem by Anacreon which describes the loving care lavished on his pet dove; it drank from his cup, ate from his hand, flew around the house and slept on his lyre. In Thomas Moore's translation, which begins: 'Tell me why, my sweetest dove', he describes the dialogue between the bird, which is carrying a message from his master to his beloved, and an inquisitive crow: 'I bear songs of passion through the air'. A later summary by the Greek philosopher Aristotle of the bird's characteristics shows clearly that he was familiar with it in many aspects:

> *Its song is a mournful plaint; it lacks gall; it continually kisses; it flies in flocks; it does not live from plunder; it collects the better seeds; it does not feed on corpses; it nests in the holes of rocks; it sits on streams in order to see the shadows of the hawk which it can then quickly avoid; it has twin young.*

Away from these literary sources, more concrete early evidence is found in the gold-foil ornaments discovered at Mycenae in 1500 BC, also a much later painted terracotta model from Apulia in Italy (*see opposite*). Several early Greek coins depicting the bird in flight at about this period can also be found.

Gold-foil ornaments from Mycenae, c.1500 BC. (National Archaeological Museum, Athens)

(left) Terracotta model of a dove, from Apulia, c.300-250 BC.
(Barbara Frears)
(right) Two early Greek coins depicting doves, from the 4th century BC.

In many early cultures of Mesopotamia in the eastern Mediterranean the image of the Great Mother Goddess was deeply embedded. Her successor was the Greek goddess Aphrodite who became the Roman Venus, both of whom shared the dove symbol (*see page 8*). In her early days in Greece she inherited the titles Queen of Heaven and Earth and Sky, also goddess of Nature and sometimes of Sea and Battle but she relinquished several of these titles over the years so that eventually in Roman times she occupied a relatively minor role and became known as goddess of love in both its sensuous and chaste forms. Nevertheless the bird was still offered up as sacrifice in the temple in Roman times as Ovid says in his *Fasti*: 'Taken from her mate the white dove is often burned on Idalian hearths'.

Venus is seen in her chariot drawn by doves, with helmeted soldiers in the foreground re-presenting Mars. (The British Library, Ms Harley 4425, fol.138)

Another Greek goddess Demeter, who became the Roman Ceres, the corn goddess, shared not only the dove symbol but the snake. Athena, the Roman Minerva, goddess of wisdom, is also occasionally depicted holding a dove.

The mare-headed Demeter holding a dove and fish, with snakes on her neck. (Barbara Frears)

(above) Athena with her dove. (Barbara Frears)

A lesser figure in the classical pantheon was Eros or Cupid; he was subordinate to Venus as an instigator of sexual love and finally played the part of a wayward, winged youth who shot arrows of infatuation and desire at random into his victims.

Oracles were originally delivered by the Earth or Mother Goddess but early patriarchal invaders made a point of seizing her shrines and installing their own priests, occasionally retaining the existing priestesses. These ancient oracular places were often centres of tree worship and dedicated to the woodland goddess Dione who became known as the triple goddess of the dove and oak cult and legendary mother of Aphrodite. Later, as at Dodona in Greece, these places were dedicated to the worship of the great god Zeus (Roman Jupiter or Jove) who was head of the Olympian family. The mention in an

(above) Eros (Cupid) riding a dove.

early text of 'Zeus's sweet acorn' indicates that the fruits of the oak trees in the sacred groves of the shrines might have been offered on the altars. The doves in the trees are thought to have contributed to the successful prophecy by analysis of their behaviour, particularly the sound of their cooing and the patterns of their flight; but their homing ability may also have played a part.

(above) Early Greek coin showing doves in trees at the oracle of Zeus at Dodona. (Barbara Frears)

In the legend from Dodona several early writers claimed that a spring flowed from the roots of an ancient oak on the site. The water or murmurings from this together with a pair of oracular doves which spoke with a human voice, possibly the 'dove priestesses', contributed toward the powers of prophecy. Water being a primeval need in nature, it is not surprising that sources such as rivers, springs and wells were regarded as sacred in earliest times. In the classical world the Roman goddess Juturna, mother of fertility, springs and fountains, fulfilled this role. It is said that doves were her messengers and she was herself sometimes depicted as a dove. In early Iranian culture the goddess Anahita was similarly linked with water and although also associated with warlike characteristics she was later worshipped with the dove.

In Celtic religion, during its survival in Roman Gaul, the well-known sculptures of the 'Dove-Deity' discovered in the last century at Alesia, Cote-d'or, illustrate the connection between springs, the bird and deity. In several examples two facing doves are depicted perching on the shoulders of a male deity. In another, a male of military appearance, wearing a tunic,

bears above and behind his shoulders two facing doves perched on oak garlands bearing acorns – a possible link with Dodona? It is claimed that these represent a certain Spring-deity of the Celtic pantheon on account of the close and intimate association which exists between doves and springs.

The 'Dove Deity' from Alesia with two pigeons sitting on his shoulders.

35

The Greek historian and geographer Strabo refers to 'oracular doves being observed for purposes of augury'. He also mentions the custom of the early Etruscans of releasing pigeons on the Mediterranean coast to signal the arrival of tunny fish shoals to nearby fishermen.

Rome started as a small cluster of villages, the Etruscans having been expelled from the region in the 6th century BC. The first temple for the worship of Venus was built in 295 BC on the coast south of Rome while another was later erected on the summit of Mount Eryx in Sicily (present-day Erice), remains of which exist today. The Romans called the doves 'pets of Aphrodite' and it is claimed that they first learned about the domestic pigeon from the Greeks at Eryx.

There are several allusions to the birds by Roman writers in the first century. Pliny the Elder, for example, writes in his *Natural History*:

> *Many people have quite a mania for pigeons, building turrets for them on house roofs and tracing the pedigree of single birds.*

(above) Bas-relief of a Roman domestic scene with two doves and a dog.

Columella endorses this by writing of those who spend large sums of money on buying pigeons for the sake of 'owning what delights and amuses them'. This can be seen in the scenes of domestic life of the times.

(left) Domestic scene painted on a Roman vase, with female figures, a cat and a dove. (British Museum, Department of Greek and Roman Antiquities)

A further example and possibly a memorial, is known as 'The Boy Successus' who holds his pet white pigeon; a duck stands beside him and the nearby pomegranate, sometimes a symbol of death, may be an indication that he had died.

The well-known mosaic of doves resting on the edge of a bronze basin, discovered at Hadrian's villa, Tivoli, is an image now known as Pliny's Pigeons because the mosaic had been mentioned by Pliny the Elder.

*(above) A Pompeian wall-painting showing 'The Boy Successus',
so-called because the words 'puer successus' were inscribed beside his head. (Barbara Frears)*

*(below) A mosaic of doves from Hadrian's Villa at Tivoli.
(Archivio Fotografico dei Musei Capitolini, Rome)*

The pigeon in a quite different role is portrayed at the Villa Imperiale in Sicily which was built between the second and fourth centuries. The scene in

the mosaic is called the Prize-giving and is a parody of one in the main building portraying the chariot races of the Circus Maximus in Rome.

It is probable that rough forms of dovecote would have been common in Rome as in other parts of the Mediterranean at an early date. The Greek Dio-

Pigeons pulling a chariot in the mosaic from the Villa Imperiale.

dorus Siculus, writing in the 1st century BC, described a mud-built structure with a thatched roof, probably similar to the one depicted in the well-known mosaic at Palestrina (*see p.26*). Varro writing a little earlier gives details of a dovecote with a domed roof and adds that there were many others in Rome, Florence and the countryside and that a single cote often contained 5,000 birds. On a minor scale a panel of pigeon flight holes has been discovered in the ruins of Pompeii (*shown right*).

Confirmation that the birds were bred for the table appears in a cookery book

The Runt, drawn by J.C. Lyell in 1872.

written by the Roman gourmet Apicius in the time of the Emperor Tiberius. It includes recipes for roast and boiled pigeon squabs and recommends boning the birds before cooking. The breed of pigeon known today as the Runt was mentioned by Pliny and was also called the Roman Banquet Pigeon; it is one of the largest breeds of the bird and has been extensively bred for the table.

In Italy the tradition of dovecote building was revived at the time of the Renaissance when buildings of impressive size and elegance were constructed. These included villas designed by Andrea Palladio in the 16th century in which pairs of dovecotes were situated on each side, equidistantly and connected by covered arcades. Many of these have been preserved.

Villa Emo in the Veneto, Northern Italy, designed by Andrea Palladio, showing one of the matching dovecote towers with its entry holes. (Paul Hansell)

Today there are a few other surviving examples from this and later periods, particularly around Bologna, as well as several plain square pigeon-towers in the Veneto, Lombardy, Tuscany and Campania.

Models of three surviving Renaissance-style dovecotes: (left) Manzoli; (centre) Isolani; (right) Rusconi, near Bologna.

In Apulia, in southern Italy, an unusual variation consists of an upper tower rising above the lower ground floor; it has exterior nesting niches, with the interior being used for other purposes.

An early, possibly Etruscan, example of a dovecote is to be found at Orvieto in Umbria. This city sits on a plateau of tufa rock out of which an underground labyrinth of wells, wine cellars, silos, shrines, cisterns and aqueducts was carved. There is also an extensive 'dovecote' area, situated at the edge of the cliffs, with openings for the pigeons to come and go to their nesting holes.

Although there are references to pigeons and doves in ancient Greece there is little evidence of dovecote building until the 13th century. At this period wealthy Venetians took over the Cycladic islands to establish ports for their ships on trade routes between Venice and the Dardanelles. During this occupation, which lasted for 400 years, monasteries, castles and chapels were built, a few remains of which are still to be found. On the island of Tinos, dovecotes were also erected and many are preserved today. In spite of being a legacy from the Italians they are said to have been built in the Greek style. In appearance they certainly display a wide variety of external decorative features which incorporate many traditional motifs of popular Greek art.

(above) A dovecote near Foggia, in Apulia, with nesting niches on the outside.

(right) Part of the 'colombaio' in the undergound city at Orvieto showing nesting holes cut out of the tufa rock.

Dovecotes on the island of Tinos.

Many of the earliest Greek fables have been attributed to Aesop, writing in the 6th century BC, the tradition being preserved in following centuries by word of mouth: they were translated into Latin verse in the reign of Augustus. Their earliest purpose was to teach rhetoric and ethics, and also to instil simple lessons of prudence. The purpose of many was to show that humans with all their wisdom and folly often behave like birds and animals. Earlier versions contain allusions to Zeus but later there is a Christian overlay. One example attributed to Aesop is the tale of the dove which rescues a drowning ant and is later spared when the ant stings a fowler intent on killing the bird; the moral drawn being 'one good turn deserves another'. In another fable the main characters recall an ancient association in the natural world. It tells of a snake which inadvertently warns a dove that it is being pursued by a hunter, hence 'Even our worst enemies may help us without meaning to'.

15th-century woodcut of the fable of the Fowler, Dove and Ant. The ant is seen on the fowler's leg.

41

One popular fable is based on the instinct of birds of prey to attack domesticated pigeons. In an example named 'The Kite, Hawk and Pigeons', the birds are supposed to have sought protection from their persecutor, the kite, by installing the hawk, which merely exchanged one hazard for another.

The Dove and the Serpent, drawn by Heidi Holden. (from Aesop's Fables, Macmillan, 1981) *The Kite, Hawk and Pigeons. (The British Library, Ms C i a 5)*

There is some evidence that the pigeon was used as a messenger in the ancient classical world; Anacreon sent a poem carried by the bird to his beloved. In the Roman world Ovid who died in the first century writes of the pigeon dyed purple which was sent back from the Olympic Games to carry news of the success of one particular participant. In England, two millennia later, away supporters of football matches also used the birds to carry home news as the game progressed. At the original Olympic Games founded by the Greeks in 776 BC the liberation of white doves symbolised the sacred armistice which prohibited all warfare during the festival. When the Games were revived in the 1890s the tradition continued until the tragic accident at Seoul in 1988 when the doves flew up into the Olympic flame and were burned to death. Subsequently, symbolic images have been substituted but with diminishing emphasis. However, the Peace Statue (*shown right*), copied from a Greek original of 450 BC, which now stands at the headquarters of the Olympic Committee in Lausanne, is a prominent reminder of the custom.

While pigeon racing is popular in Italy today, and there is an Italian Pigeon Federation, the sport of *triganieri* was enjoyed in Italy centuries ago having been introduced from the East. A flight or 'Kit' was released simultaneously with the birds from a nearby loft or lofts. After mingling together the birds were signalled down by their owners with flags or whistles and were then rewarded with tit-bits, any strange bird being taken captive.

Further Reading

anon. (1824), *Gesta Romaorum: Deeds of the Romans or Entertaining Moral Stories*, trans. Charles Swan, London

Aesop (1866), *The Fables of Aesop*, trans. S. Croxall and G.F. Townsend, Warne, London

Aesop (1981), *Aesop's Fables*, illustrated by Heidi Holder, Macmillan, London

Aristotle (1862), *Aristotle's History of Animals*, trans. Richard Cresswell, Book IX, Bohn's Classical Library, London

Baring, Anne & Cashford, Jules (1993), *The Myth of the Goddess*, Penguin Books, Harmondsworth

Cook, A.O. (1914-40), *Zeus, A Study in Ancient Religion*, Vols.I, II (2), III, Cambridge University Press, Cambridge

Daremberg, C.V. & Saglio, E. (1873-87), *Dictionnaire des Antiquités Grecques et Romains*, 5 vols, Hachette, Paris

Grigson, G. (1978), *The Goddess of Love*, Quartet Books, London

James, E.O. (1951), *The Cult of the Mother Goddess*, Thames & Hudson, London

Klingender, F.D. (1971), *Animals in Art and Thought to the End of the Middle Ages*, Routledge & Kegan Paul, London

La Fontaine, J. de (1884), *The Fables of La Fontaine*, trans. Robert Thomson, Nimmo & Bain, London

Pliny the Elder (1940), *Natural History*, trans. H. Rackham, Harvard University Press, Harvard (Mass.)

The Pigeon in the Muslim World

The recent resurgence of interest in pigeon racing in Kuwait, with the prospect of extending the interest elsewhere in the Middle East, is a reminder of the important role played by pigeons in the Muslim world in the past. Muhammad is credited with having introduced the pigeon known as the Arabian Laugher. Known for its unusual 'voice' it was reported centuries later in 1881 as having been seen in India. It is still bred today in many regions. Early in the last century it was reported that the thousands of pigeons which were to be seen at the

shrine of Muhammad at Medina were known as the 'Prophet's Birds'. The bird known as the Muhammad was first described in England in the 17th century as having come from Turkey but its origins and lineage were later disputed. Rather, this bird, also known as the Damascene, is believed to have been named after the prophet. The bird known as the Wattle Pigeon was also bred in this part of the world; the English Carrier eventually came from this group.

(above) The Mahomet Pigeon, drawn by J.C. Lyell in 1879.

As I have already shown, early archaeological finds depict the pigeon as the symbol of the Great Mother Goddess, the supreme deity of the Near East, Eastern Mediterranean and Ancient Greece. Tracing references to the bird in the ancient world of Islam depends on more slender threads of evidence and involves much interweaving and overlapping between the various other religions. Random glimpses in myths and legends can also be revealing.

(left) The Blue Carrier Cock, painted by J.W. Ludlow, from Robert Fulton's Illustrated Book of Pigeons, 1895.

It must be remembered that of the three monotheistic religions, Judaism and Christianity, both known as 'People of the Book', shared Old Testament beliefs with Islam, including the account of the Flood, Noah's Ark and the dove. One early shared legend tells of the pigeon which was trained to seek corn placed in Muhammad's ear, the intention being to give the impression that the prophet thereby received a divine message from on high. Pope Gregory and other divines were also shown in many works of art being similarly inspired.

(above) A pigeon sitting on Pope Gregory's shoulder. Note the scribe on the left, recording the scene. (Barbara Frears)

The Emir of Cairo's tent, from Georg Ebers' Aegypten in Bild und Wort, 1879.

Another story of the 5th and 6th centuries concerns the foundation of the city of Cairo. An Emir, involved in the Islamic conquest of Egypt, returning to his tent in the desert after a long absence, refrained from pulling it down as intended as a pair of doves had built their nest on top (*shown left*). He declared:

> God forbid that Muslims should deny hospitality to a living creature of God which made its home trusting in the shadow of his hospitality.

He returned to live in the tent and founded a new town, 'Fosta,' which means tent. This eventually became 'Mist' and, later, Cairo.

Unlike places of worship in the West which contain images and other forms of artistic expression, these are not found in mosques where the worship of idols is forbidden. Instead they often display the supreme form of Islamic art,

calligraphy. A fine example is the dove as a symbol of peace, the image being made up of the letters meaning peace (*shown left*). Of more substantial form is a striking 11th-century incense-burner, thought to be from Sicily, which is in the form of a typical pigeon, probably the Scandaroon variety, having a markedly curved beak.

An 11th-century bronze incense-burner, possibly produced in Sicily. (Aga Khan Trust for Culture)

In the early days of the Muslim faith, precious materials such as gold, silver, pearls, coral and rubies were regarded as symbols of creation. The use of jewellery was mentioned in the *Hadith*, which was a summary of the Prophet Muhammad's sayings and was interpreted in different ways. In some versions it was regarded as being materialistic and Muslims were not only forbidden from manufacturing it but prohibited from wearing silver or gold next to the body. In another, an edict stated that if any jewellery is worn it must be removed before prayers out of respect for Muhammad. There is later evidence that some caliphs and sultans wore heavy jewellery including rings on their fingers possibly in emulation of Byzantine and Chinese emperors.

From earliest times, nature played a role in the design of Islamic jewellery although it has also been claimed that the basis of it was a combination of calligraphy, geometry and floral patterns. The symbolism of the time was also based on the Garden of Eden, and the 'Kissing Birds of Paradise' are exemplified by birds such as peacocks and doves. An 11th- to 12th-century Iranian example of a pair of gold earrings depicts two facing birds, probably doves, set within a crescent. These symbolic facing birds represent an ancient device, occasionally using other creatures, which originated in many early cultures including the Near East and the classical world. An elaborate gold pendant framing the same symbol also comes from Iran and dates from the same period. Later, smaller ornamental decorations, dating from the 17th-century Mughal

Gold earrings and pendant from Iran, 11th-12th centuries. (Metropolitan Museum of Art)

period, include the so-called 'elements' for turban ornaments which are made from emerald and set with rubies, and also a bejewelled gold finger ring with a bobbing bird, which is almost certainly a pigeon (*shown overleaf*).

Turban ornament in the form of a dove.

47

17th-century Mughal gold ring with dove decoration.

Muslim poets have always been skilled in writing verse of all kinds. In the 11th century, the work known as the *Ring of the Dove* (a treatise on the art and practice of Arab love) by Ibn Hazim of Cordoba appeared at the time when Moorish Spain was enjoying a prosperous and elegant culture. It explains the method by which a lover sends a message to his beloved thus: 'Old Noah chose a dove to be his faithful messenger'.

Rumi, another poet writing in 1260 AD, pin-points the characteristic natural habitat of the bird: 'O my dove that art in the cleft of the rocks', and also makes a figurative mention of the bird:

'You are peace that descends with the dove'. A Persian manuscript, *The Conference of the Birds* by the 12th-century poet Farid ud-Dinn Attar, is an allegorical fable of the birds' search for their king, but in the end they find themselves. The pigeon is greeted by their leader: 'Salutations, O pigeon', and mention is also made of the turtle dove. A 15th-century illustrated version includes the beautiful 'The Concourse of Birds' in which several doves are depicted.

A capriccio of fancy pigeons depicted beside a travelling dovecote, from a Mughal miniature dated c.1670. (copyright British Museum)

In north-west Afghanistan an impressive early example of the symbolic use of the pigeon is found at Mazar-i-Sharif which lies close to the ancient Silk Road. This was the site of the shrine of the prophet Ali-bin-Talib, founded in 1136 AD. He was the cousin and son-in-law of the prophet Muhammad and is considered to be his successor by his Shiite followers. This has resulted in the crucial split between the Shia and Sunni branches of the faith which has continued through the ages. The site of the shrine was destroyed by the Mongols in 1226 AD but rebuilding took place in the late 15th century as the beautiful Blue Mosque which still contains the shrine of Ali together with others. It draws thousands of Shiite pilgrims, especially during the festival of the New Year, and was well-described recently by the writer Colin Thubron during his travels along the Silk Road. The photographs below and overleaf show the mosque with a huge flock of white doves which are believed to be offerings or blessings to Ali. An ancient legend relates the belief that if a strange coloured pigeon joins the flock it will become white overnight.

There was a long tradition in the Arab world of using Carrier Pigeons to send messages, both in Baghdad in the 7th century and in Moorish Spain in the 11th and 12th centuries. The birds were also used for sport, not only as racing pigeons but in *triganieri* as well. In 16th-century India the Emperor Akbar, a very keen pigeon fancier, enjoyed a variation on the theme in a pursuit with the birds which he called 'love play'.

(left) A 17th-century woodcut depicting messenger birds in the Near East with the messages tied round their necks.

(below) The sport of 'triganieri' as shown in an Arabic treatise. (The British Library, Ms IO Persian 4811, fol.4)

(below) The Carrier Pigeon, painted by J.C. Lyell, c.1890.

(left) Modern Iznik ceramic model of a pigeon from Istanbul.
(right) Ceramic and metal pigeon ashtray from present-day Morocco.

Today, politicians and writers are urging the need for religions of the world to learn to co-exist in the name of peace. This coincides with our age of consumerism in which the dove symbol, either alone or carrying an olive branch, is commonplace in publicity and promotion. It is however ironic to see a current image from the Near East depicting the birds wearing helmets (*shown right*). It is a sad reflection on the symbol of peace that it should be used in this discordant way.

Further Reading

Abu al-Fazl (1873), *The Aín Akbarí*, trans. H. Blochman, Calcutta
Ahmed, Akbar S. (1993), *Living Islam*, BBC Books, London
Al-Sabbāgh, Mīkhā'īl (1805), *La Colombe messagère plus rapide que l'éclair plus prompte que la nue*, trans. A.I. Silvestre de Sacy, Imprimerie Impériale, Paris
'Attār, Farīd al-Dīn (1961), *The Conference of the Birds: Mantiq Ut-Tair*, trans. C.S. Nott, Routledge & Kegan Paul, London
Burton, Richard (1893), *Personal Narrative of a Pilgrimage to Al-Madinah and Meccah*, Tylston and Edwards, London
Matar, N.I. (1992), *Islam for Beginners*, Writers and Readers Publishing, New York
Musavi, Sayid Muhammad Valih (c.1770), *Kabutarnama* (The History of Pigeons), Persian ms Islamic 4811, Oriental & India Office Collections, British Library, London
Price, Judith (2008), *Masterpieces of Ancient Jewelry*, Running Press, Philadelphia (Pa.)
Shah, Idries (1968), *Caravan of Dreams*, Octagon Press, London
Thubron, C. (2006), *Shadow of the Silk Road*, Chatto & Windus, London
Zaehner, R.C. (1961), *The Dawn and Twilight of Zoroastrianism*, Weidenfeld & Nicolson, London

The Pigeon in India

It is now generally believed that in prehistoric times the earliest Indian people came from Africa migrating thence to Southern Asia and finally arriving in India. The introduction of crops in about 7000 BC to these primitive hunter-gatherers was followed by the eventual domestication of animals. Recent writers state that hens, ducks and geese were amongst the fowl included but pigeons are not specifically mentioned although it seems certain that they would have followed the introduction of wheat crops. The later development of cities took place largely in Northern India in the Indus valley.

The Blue Rock pigeon (*Columbia livia*) occurs naturally all over India from Sri Lanka to the Himalayas. Its original habitat was mainly on coastal cliffs and inland mountains but it also had the unusual habit of nesting in the walls of well-shafts and in underground water channels. Nowadays, like their cousins in other parts of the world, the pigeons make their home in the high nooks and crannies of mosques, minarets, temples, churches and other buildings in the towns.

Many of these feral birds, as elsewhere, are descended from domesticated ancestors. A decade or so ago it was reported that pigeons were being maintained by cooperative effort at Dadar in Bombay where a dovecote stood in the middle of a group of buildings comprising a Muslim mosque, a Hindu temple and a Christian church. It was a square structure on a pole and housed about 40 birds which were looked after by the local people of all faiths.

In the course of its long history, the Indus region of India was repeatedly overrun by waves of invaders from the north. The first to be identified were the Aryans who appeared in the middle of the second millennium BC. The *Rig Veda*, written in Sanskrit, is the most ancient and important hymn to be dedicated to the Aryan deities and is believed to date from 1500-1200 BC. Its mythological origin based on the Creation of the Universe is said to have been from the great god Brahma's eastern mouth. In one hymn the dove or pigeon is named the Dove of Death, also the messenger of the god of death.

Writing in the early 20th century about the role of the pigeon in ancient times, Charles Sibillot referred to the interior of the Buddhist temple at Mount Abu, near Adaipur in Northern India, where two pairs of doves surmount the sacred sanctuary.

In another work, the *Jataka*, also known as stories of the Buddha's former births, one of a number of fables relates that the Buddha in the form of a pigeon was happily housed and fed in a dwelling only to be ousted by a greedy crow.

Two pairs of doves above the inner sanctuary of the Buddhist temople at Mount Abu. (Barbara Frears)

In later religious development the Hindu Trinity comprised Brahma the Creator together with the Hindu gods Vishnu the Preserver and Shiva the Destroyer, accompanied by innumerable other deities both male and female. One legend relates that Shiva at one time found some of his followers so exasperating that he turned them into pigeons; they have haunted his shrines and temples ever since, hoping for release. The Goddess Saraswati, wife of Brahma, was credited with having invented the Sanskrit language, and also of possessing great powers of imagination and invention; she was adored as patroness of the fine arts. She is often depicted riding on a goose, parrot or peacock.

The custom of depicting deities in a 'bird-vehicle' seems to have been prevalent and Vishnu can be found seated on the mythical bird Garuda with the lesser god Kamadeva riding on a pigeon. The latter deity was known as the god of love, representing the longing for happiness and the fulfilment of desires, and was often shown carrying a bow of buzzing bees and flower-tipped arrows symbolising the five senses.

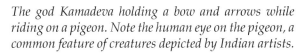

The god Kamadeva holding a bow and arrows while riding on a pigeon. Note the human eye on the pigeon, a common feature of creatures depicted by Indian artists.

The great Sanskrit epic, the *Mahabharatha*, written around the 3rd century AD, includes folklore, philosophy and legend, and relates the story of a king who sacrificed a limb for a pigeon who had sought his protection from a hawk. The hawk argued his case for preying on the bird as being part of his diet and of his nature. The king, finding himself in a dilemma, offered to cut pieces of his own flesh equal to the weight of the intended victim. The moral of the tale is drawn at the beginning by two gods who are testing the wisdom and virtue of the king. The fable concludes on a happy note even though the moral message is rather uncertain. It is, of course, based on the instinctive natural behaviour of the birds which was noted by Aristotle and later incorporated into fables in the west.

The fables of Pilpay, an ancient Indian philosopher, were also written in Sanskrit in the 3rd century and translated for the Mughal emperor Akbar in the 16th century. One story, entitled 'The Raven, the Rat and the Pigeons' or 'The Advantage of the United Action of Friends', is possibly an early allusion to team spirit.

Representation of the fable of the king who sacrificed his arm for a pigeon. Note the reference to the Jain bird hospital in Delhi at the bottom. (photograph by Amar Grover)

It relates the tale of some pigeons trapped in a fowler's net who are exhorted by their leader to work together to loosen it so that they can fly away although still entangled in it. Having landed out of harm's way the leader asks a rat to help him to 'free my companions before me'. Admiring his selflessness the rat nibbles a hole in the net and frees them all. As a sub-plot the cunning raven plays the role of a hidden observer who, wishing to discover the secret of the rat's cooperation, but being unaware of the rat's respect for the leader pigeon, fails to gain a similar confidence.

Pilpay's fable of 'The Raven, the Rat and the Pigeons'. Above left, the pigeons entangled in the net, watched by the fowler. Above right, the pigeons being freed by the friendly rat. Below, the rat nibbling at the net to free the pigeons, watched by the raven. (above, The British Library, Johnson 54, Nos.19 & 20; below, Bodleian Library, University of Oxford, Ms Pococke 400, fol.82v)

Several early bestiaries in the west, which were allegorical legends based on animals or birds, refer to the tree called Peridexion or Perindens which grew in India and produced sweet fruits on which pigeons and doves fed. It seems probable that these birds might have been a variety of fruit pigeon rather than the rock pigeon which doesn't eat fruit – nevertheless, the message of the story was that the doves were protected from their enemy, the dragon which lurked on the ground below, as long as they stayed in the tree or within its shade. A suitable Christian interpretation for this tale was adopted in the west.

ne postquam accepis spm scm boc est spualem columbam intelligibilem de celo descendentem et manentem supre fons tuaf ab etnitate. alienuf a pre et filio et spu sco. et diaco terin terimat.i. diabolus. Nam si tu habeaf spm scm non potest i

The Peridexion or Perindens tree. Doves are seen perching on the branches and on the dragons' tails below. (Queen Mother Library, University of Aberdeen, Ms 24, fol.65)

A later and contrasting illustration in an Indian manuscript of the Mughal period represents the Islamic belief that the throne of God has four pillars, each supported by an angel holding a canopy decorated with rows of pigeons.

The Sikh religion was founded in the Punjab at the end of the 16th century as a strictly monotheistic faith but which contained elements of Hinduism and Islam. Sikhs believe that the dove is a symbol of peace, harmony and goodwill and some also think that it is linked with reincarnation. At the end of the 17th century, their leader Guru Govind Singh created a military group in defence of the faith. He is often rep-

Rows of doves on a canopy held above the throne of God. (Bodleian Library, University of Oxford, Ms Pers. d.29, fol.66r)

resented with what is called the Holy Dove, believed to symbolise inspiration and to demonstrate that although he was a warrior he was also a man of peace.

There is little doubt that in India since earliest times, as in many other parts of the world, the pigeon has been bred as symbol, sacrifice, source of food and not least as messenger but the time of the Mughal emperors in the 16th century saw the greatest development of interest in the bird. The emperor Akbar was an enlightened ruler whose wisdom, religious tolerance, love of nature and en-

Guru Govind Singh on horseback, holding the Holy Dove. (courtesy of Gursh Salona)

couragement of art and architecture brought about a flowering of Indian civilisation. He had the reputation of being a keen sportsman but as well as hawking and hunting he kept menageries, aviaries and dovecotes. His pigeons, to whom he was devoted, accompanied him on his travels, being transported in small cotes as seen in 17th-century Mughal miniature paintings (*shown below*).

(Fitzwilliam Museum, Cambridge)   *(The British Library, Ms ADD OR 3129, fol.31)*

As one record says:

> At the time of departure and breaking-up of the camp, the pigeons will follow, the cots being carried by bearers. Sometimes they [the birds] will alight and take rest for a while, then rise again.

Chronicles relate that Akbar kept 20,000 pigeons at one time and was regarded as an expert on breeding fancy varieties although the truth may well be that he was building on an earlier tradition. Today, many varieties, including the Fantails, Lahores and Jacobins, are believed to have originated in India. No doubt he also used the birds as messengers, already a common practice in the Near East, and enjoyed the sport of 'pigeon flying' which he called 'love play'.

(left) Domestic dove-keeping in India, from a contemporary miniature. Note the dovecote at ground level and the pole with a platform on which the birds could alight.

(right) Keeping pigeons for pleasure, again with a ground-level dovecote. The enlarged detail shows a pair of birds mating.
(Bodleian Library, University of Oxford, Ms Douce or. a.3, fol.10r)

(left) A roof-top dovecote on a Mughal palace. (Barbara Frears)

(right) A floral fantasy Deccani painting showing pigeons amid a riot of flowers.

Shah Jehan, the 5th Mughal emperor, came to the throne in 1628 and was responsible for the creation of the Taj Mahal as a monument to his beloved second wife. A depiction of them both in which she holds a white dove (*shown right*) follows the tradition of keeping the birds as domestic pets.

Nearer the present day the news that the Indian Police Pigeon Service in Orissa had recently to be discontinued confirms that the custom in the recent past of using the birds as messengers had carried on over the centuries, possibly continuing since the time when the Caliph of Baghdad established a service in the 12th century. Today in India satellite communication has taken over.

Writing over the past two decades William Dalrymple provides glimpses into the world of the pigeon in India, past and present. In describing a visit

to a Muslim household in Delhi where pigeons were housed on the roof he was intrigued to learn that the birds were trained to take part in the popular sport of pigeon flying. This appears to resemble *triganieri* or might be a variant of Akbar's 'love play' sport. He refers to the earlier days of Mughal rule when cock-fighting and pigeon-flying were popular pursuits, as well as the custom among high-born Muslim ladies of keeping pigeons in their gardens. He also includes a useful mention of present-day Indian terminology. The pigeon is called 'Kabooter' while 'Kabooter baz' means pigeon-flying and 'Golay' is a racing pigeon.

The Fantail

The Sherajee or Lahore

A selection of Indian pigeon varieties

The Jacobin

The Mookee

Further Reading

anon. (1895-1913), *The Jātaka, or Stories of the Buddha's former Births*, Vols. I & II,
    trans. R. Chalmers and W.H. Rouse, Cambridge University Press, Cambridge
Abu al-Fazl (1873), *The Aín Akbarí*, trans. H. Blochman, Calcutta
Dallapiccola, A.L. (2002), *Dictionary of Hindu Lore and Legend*,
    Thames and Hudson, London & New York
Dalrymple, William (2002), *White Mughals*, Harper Collins, London
Gascoigne, B. (1971), *The Great Moguls*, Jonathan Cape, London
Grover, Amar (1999), 'Broken Wings, Healing Hands', *The Independent*, London
Moor, E. (1864), *The Hindu Pantheon*, J. Higginbotham, Madras
Ions, Veronica (1968), *Egyptian Mythology*, Hamlyn, London
James, T.G.H. (1969), *Myths and Legends of Ancient Egypt*, Hamlyn, London
O'Flaherty, Wendy D. (1975), *Hindu Myths: a Source Book*, Penguin Books, Harmondsworth
Shattuck, C. (1999), *Hinduism*, Routledge, London
Sibillot, C. (1916) *Lo Sport Colombofilo negli antichi tempi*, trans. R. Sacerdoti, Modena
Zimmer, H. (1962), *Myths and Symbols in Indian Art and Architecture*, ed. J. Campbell,
    Harper and Bros., New York

The Pigeon in China

Very little is known today in the west about the world of the pigeon in China. Traces in the history and mythology of the past are few and far between, and often fragmentary, but confirm that the bird, as in other parts of the world, has been used for centuries as symbol, source of food and messenger. One of the earliest brief allusions to it is to be found in an anonymous Chinese poem dating from 700 BC:

> *My lord has gone away to serve the king,*
> *The pigeons homing at the set of the sun*
> *Are side by side upon the courtyard wall,*
> *And far away I hear the herdsman call.*

Centuries later the ceramic model of a farmstead, excavated from a tomb at Chang-Chou near Honan and dating from the 1st century, confirms that domestication had already become established. Two towers standing at the corners of the courtyard have square flight-holes which are thought to give access to an inner pigeon loft. An adjoining lower building on which three birds are perched is also claimed to have had a similar use. Today in China pigeons are still popular on the menu, either roasted or stewed.

Courtyard in Honan. Note the pigeons sitting on the lower roof-top. (Barbara Frears)

Recently there was considerable interest in the exhibition at the British Museum on 'The First Emperor' who ruled from 221-201 BC. The exhibition was based on the discovery in 1914 of his burial site whose chief importance is the amazing find of large numbers of terracotta warriors in the excavation. Nearby, a sacrificial pit was unearthed containing the remains of bronze swans, wild geese and cranes which together with several buried musicians were intended to provide entertainment for the Emperor in his after-life. Although no pigeons were discovered here, on the site of a local village which supplied tiles and bricks, a small decoration was found in the form of a bird, most probably a pigeon (*shown right*).

Nestorian Christian missionaries travelling from Persia along the Silk Road arrived in China in the 1st century. A collection of bronze seals known as Nestorian crosses, some of which are believed to date from this period, have been discovered and now form the basis of a collection in the museum of the University of Hong Kong. In practice they were used to mark bread, clay or wax while an unusual account tells of the Mongol shepherds who secured the doors of their dwellings with a seal when they departed to move their sheep up onto the hills. A mixture of Nestorian and Buddhist influences are believed to explain the symbolism involved in the crosses. The swastika which appears on some is thought to represent the sun symbol in Buddhism while the bird, almost certainly a pigeon, could represent the Holy Spirit of Christianity or the Buddhist symbol of good fortune.

Three bronze Nestorian crosses from the 1st century. (centre: Museum of East Asian Art, Bath)

At this period, before the arrival of the Christians, the chief religions were Buddhism, Taoism and Confucianism, the latter said to be a book of rules rather than a religion. The related observances in the Chinese pantheon were said to be so unlimited that there was scarcely a being or thing which had not at some time been propitiated or worshipped. An early goddess known as Guan or Kuan Min was introduced in the 5th century and worshipped chiefly in South China. She is known as the goddess of mercy and bestower of and protector of children. Several depictions show her with a white lotus flower symbolising purity and a dove representing peace and fecundity. Also linked with her is a vase symbolising the water of wisdom and compassion; a book or scroll of prayers; the yoni, the female genital symbol; and the so-called pearls of illumination.

The Goddess Guan or Kuan Min. By her right shoulder is a parcel of books and on her left a dove holding a necklace. (Barbara Frears)

A quite different custom in the Han dynasty was to present elderly people with a jade-stone sceptre having a dove at the tip. It was also known as a 'pigeon-staff' which symbolised protracted longevity and also the quaint hope that the individual's digestion would continue to be as good as that of the bird.

By contrast, in general the Chinese considered the dove to be eminently stupid and lascivious but did grant that it had qualities of faithfulness, impartiality and filial duty, the latter perhaps exemplified by the observation that pigeons feed their squabs with pigeon's milk, a feature unique in the avian world.

A Buddhist legend, also familiar in Hinduism as described in the last chapter, relates the story of the king who sacrificed a limb for a pigeon which had sought his protection from a hawk. A different legend in Taoism with a clearer moral lesson involved the New Year custom of presenting a number of pigeons to the governor who liberally rewarded the donors. However, this action inevitably involved the death of several birds.

A 3rd-century relief of the Buddhist legend of the King, the Hawk and the Pigeon, seen on the bottom left. (Barbara Frears)

A critic at the time remarked that kindness cannot compensate for cruelty and this was acknowledged as correct.

The Silk Road between China and the Mediterranean carried religions, custom and trades from earliest times. It was not until the 17th century, however, that large-scale transmission of ideas between Europe and the Far East arrived, chiefly in the form of Jesuit missionaries. In pursuit of their proselytising zeal they worked with the local people and introduced them to European technology, at first mainly in Canton. No doubt much was also learned from the Chinese themselves. A recent exhibition in London entitled 'Encounters' illustrated this direct contact between East and West in the years 1500 to 1800. A detail from a lacquer screen presented to an official in Canton in 1674 represents gifts being given to a Tang dynasty general on his 80th birthday (*shown below*). The presence of Europeans (who look like Orientals), is intended to flatter the recipient by implying that all the world came to China bearing gifts. Among them is a white dove being carried aloft on a tray.

During the 17th and 18th centuries a fashion for the so-called chinoiserie style influenced many aspects of interior design in the west; a decorative detail from a wooden picture frame illustrates this trend.

An 18th-century, Chinoiserie-style decoration on a wooden picture frame. (Bath Preservation Trust collection)

In the British Isles, more than a century or so ago at a time when there was keen interest and enthusiasm for breeding fancy pigeons, the author James Lyell commented: 'many curious pigeons are in the possession of Asian fanciers that we know little about'. At that time, in his 1887 work *Fancy Pigeons*, he recorded a new arrival from China named the Chinese Dewlap Pigeon (*shown right*) which he described as being blue in colour with white flights, spots on the forehead and on either side of the neck; the bird also had an enormous gullet. The Owl breed of pigeon had been bred in the UK since the 18th century but the arrival of the African Owl from Tunis was recorded by the American author W.M. Levi a hundred years later. In spite of its origin several writers believed that it really came from the East and the subsequent existence of the Chinese Owl might confirm that. The English Owl was crossed with the imported variety and apart from the rounded head-shape, the most striking characteristic of both is the marked breast frill (*see illustration opposite*). Levi deplored how little was known about Chinese pigeons and the scarcity of information in English and continental literature about them. However, his enquiries revealed the existence of three breeds which were familiar at that time in the United States. The Ring

*Two English Owl Pigeon varieties, painted by J.W. Ludlow,
from Robert Fulton's Illustrated Book of Pigeons, 1895.*

Breast, popular in Beijing and used for pigeon-whistle flying, and having the nasal tuft previously described; the Tungoon Pak used for pigeon racing and the Bloody-Red Blue Eye, the name referring to the colour of the birds' eyes; it was used for racing and squab production. In a later book written in 2000 in the USA, Alex Rawson includes several Chinese breeds which had been imported into California in 1980. Among those mentioned are the Peking Ring Breast, as described above, whose nasal tuft he calls the Prayer Crest; the Tiger Hood; the Chinese Mottle; Jade Ring Breast; Silver Tail; and many others.

*The Chinese Ring-breasted or Beak-crested Pigeon.
(inset) a drawing of the pigeon's nasal tuft.*

In China itself, an unknown writer in the Sung dynasty (960-1280) relates that pigeon rearing was very popular, some breeds being referred to as 'the Beauties of half the heavens' while apparently some people were so fascinated by the birds that they prized them more than the beauty of lovely maidens and named them the 'Winged Maidens'. A later writer in the Ming dynasty (1368-1644) refers to pigeons of beautiful shapes, 'like the Flowers of Spring'. Early in the last century the names of the birds that were sold in the Flower Market of Beijing give some idea of the pigeons' exotic appearance: 'Phoenix-headed white', 'Parrot-beaked Spotted', 'Magpie Flowers' and 'Square-edged Unicorn'.

The release of pigeons carrying little whistles and flutes is a custom believed to date from the 12th century and has been popular in Indonesia, Taiwan, Bali and China, particularly in Beijing. An extract from the *National Geographic Magazine* in 1913 explains that the custom is not, as customarily believed, to protect the birds from hungry hawks but

> *it is not the pigeon that profits from the practice but merely the human ear which feasts on wind-blown tunes and derives aesthetic pleasure from the music.*

Older Chinese describe the sound as 'heavenly music' or 'the voices of their ancestors'. The whistles, weighing only a few grams, are still made today from gourds, bamboo, light-weight wood and more recently plastic. They are usually fitted to the bird in an upright position on the two middle tail feathers near the rump. It is a curious coincidence that, quite independently of the birds, actual whistles were used to produce sound from an early date. A ceramic model of this type of device dating from the 7th to 10th century is in the form of a pigeon.

(left) Chinese pigeon whistle attached to a bird's tail. (Pitt-Rivers Museum, University of Oxford)
(right) A selection of pigeon whistles made from gourds and bamboo. (Peter Hansell)

(above left) Pigeon whistle made from a decorated gourd. (Veronica Mayhew)

(above right) Pottery whistle made in the form of a pigeon. (Museum of East Asian Art, Bath)

(right) Present-day pigeon whistles from Beijing. (Jim Jenner)

The pigeons' innate homing ability combined with its great sense of orientation has enabled it to be used for sending messages since earliest times. Salvador Bofarull claimed that the birds have been bred in China since 772 BC and that in 676 BC Arab and Indian merchants used carrier pigeons on visits to China. Centuries later there is reference to their use in carrying personal correspondence, and a description of the methods used in attaching messages to the birds' legs. More recently a report from western missionaries recorded the large number of homing pigeons that were kept in Shanghai and noted the devoted care given to them by their keepers. The birds were also used to carry trading news between towns as well as from incoming junks.

It was a short step from using the birds in this way to the sport of pigeon racing which, jumping the centuries, is becoming increasingly popular in China today. Writing in 1941 Levi mentioned several racing breeds including the Ring Breast, but it is not clear exactly where they were used at that time. Nowadays it seems that the Racing Homer from the west is generally used in the sport.

Commemorative coin from the 1988 Olympic Games in Seoul. (Barbara Frears)

During the opening ceremony of the Olympic Games the tradition of liberating a flight of white doves symbolised the sacred armistice that prohibited all warfare during the month of the games. This had become an established custom since the days of the Greeks until the tragic accident in Seoul in 1988 when birds flew into the Olympic flame and were burned to death. Subsequently a symbolic representation has been used. At Sydney in 2000 this took the form of a white dove carrying an olive branch as an image which was projected over the heads of the contestants during the final ceremony.

However, the birds have not been forgotten today although in a different role, as can be seen from a promotion for the recent Chinese Design exhibition at the Victoria and Albert Museum in London. The scene entitled 'Folded Friends' portrays a smiling girl surrounded by pigeons, but they are folded ones, designed to challenge preconceptions about China, and to emphasise that origami originated in China and Japan.

Further Reading

Burkhardt, T. (1967), *Sacred Art in East and West*, trans. Lord Northbourne,
    Perennial Books, London
Chapman, F.M. (1913), 'Chinese Pigeon Whistles', *National Geographic Magazine*, June 1913,
    Vol.23, No.6
Fulton, R. (1895), *The Illustrated Book of Pigeons*, Cassell, London
Hoose, H.P. (1938), *Peking Pigeons and Pigeon Flutes*, College of Chinese Studies, Peking
Lajard, J.B.F. (1837-49), *Recherches sue le culte, les symboles, les attributs et les monuments figurés
    de Venus en Orient et en Occident*, Bourgeois-Maze, Paris
Levi, W.M. (1941), *The Pigeon*, Levi Publishing Company, Sumpter (SC)
Li-Ch'en, Tun (1936), *Annual Customs and Festivals in Peking*, trans. D. Bodde, Henri Vetch, Peiping
Stevens, K.G. (1997), *Chinese Gods*, Collins & Brown, London
Terzani, T. (1986), *Behind the Forbidden Door: Travels in China*, Allen & Unwin, London
Williams, C.A.S. (1976), *Outlines of Chinese Symbolism and Art Motifs*,
    Dover Publications, New York

The Pigeon along the Silk Road

At one time China and Rome were the two great super-powers of the ancient world. However, their two empires were not only separated by thousands of miles of inhospitable terrain but also Rome's adversary, the Parthian Empire (247 BC-220 AD), roughly today's Iran and Iraq, intervened. The opportunities for direct communication were therefore limited. However as early as the 1st century AD silk had been introduced into Rome as shown in a fresco from Pompeii in which a mythological figure clothed in silk is portrayed. In the days of the Emperor Augustus (27 BC-14 AD) the Romans knew of the existence of the people of the Far East whom they called the Seres or Silk People in the country they named Serindia. This may have been the result of a great increase in maritime trade between India, China and Egypt which involved the exchange of goods between cosmopolitan cities of the Near and Far East. The overland Silk Road is assumed to have existed by the time of the Emperor Justinian in the 6th century when Nestorian Christian monks, who had already established bases in northern India, travelled further east and eventually arrived in China.

Among the many commodities arriving in the west from China, India and the Near East were jade, paper, ivory, precious, semi-precious stones and also religious and cultural ideas. Although pigeons are known to have been bred in China at an early date they are seldom mentioned but it is worth recording that in the days of Alexander the Great in the 4th century BC it had been claimed they were known as spoils of war. During his conquest of Persia he had also come across them when he journeyed on to India; in this way they are believed to have been introduced into Greece. However, older records show that they had arrived earlier in that country. Centuries later, at the time of the Mughal Emperor Akbar, the pigeon known there as the Lahore, and the Sherajee in Iran, were identical. This suggests that a thriving trade existed between these nations which almost certainly used the Silk Road.

In China, at the easternmost end of the Silk Road, several other religions had been established before the arrival of Christianity, mainly Buddhism, Taoism and Confucianism. One of the earliest traces of the pigeon is to be found at Dunhuang which lies west of the eastern termination. This town was established in 111 BC during the Han Empire and lies south of the Gobi desert and north of Tibet. South-east of the town, beside an oasis, are 'The Caves of the Thousand Buddhas' also known as 'The Art Gallery of the Desert'. According to an ancient stele these caves were carved from the cliffs in 698 and became a centre for Buddhist monks and other travellers along the Silk Road. They contain large

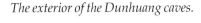
The exterior of the Dunhuang caves.

numbers of shrines decorated with murals and sculptures which reveal Chinese, Indian, Graeco-Roman and Iranian influences. Recently designated as a cultural treasure the walls and ceilings are covered with vivid paintings on a grand scale and are remarkably well preserved. Colin Thubron describes angels, lotus flowers, winged dragons, horses, human-headed birds and in one case the so-called Queen Mother of the West in a carriage drawn by phoenixes through a blizzard of falling snow. The richest and most intricate cave paintings are those of Paradise, not Buddha's hard-won Nirvana but one which the author judged to be a solace for simple people. It depicts temples, kiosks, gardens and includes a goddess on a lotus-throne. A lake is portrayed beside which is a figure leaning over a balcony releasing a flock of white doves.

In addition there is a painting of the Buddhist deity Avalokitesvara, dating from the 9th or 10th centuries, which is believed to be the work of a child. It depicts the standing two-armed deity decorated with ribbons together with a small male figure on the left thought to be the artist. Originally the deity was considered to be the goddess of mercy and compassion but was later represented as male or androgynous. One early symbol was a parrot but in this picture two birds beside the feet may well represent a pair of pigeons, which were sometimes linked with wisdom in both the east and the west.

The depiction of the goddess Avalokitesvara from Cave 17 at Dunhuang.

Going due west from Dunhuang the road travelled along the northern edge of the vast Taklamakan desert to arrive at Kuchan on the northern route of the Silk Road and once its commercial hub. North of the town lie the Kizil caves located in barren cliffs. These consist of a warren of 300 Buddhist cave temples containing many murals dating from the 3rd and 8th centuries. Unfortunately many have been damaged and others removed by westerners. One mural depicts the familiar Buddhist and Hindu legend of the hawk and the pigeon which was later absorbed into Western folklore.

A sketch of the mural at Kizil which represents the fable of the King, the Hawk and the Pigeon.

From Dunhuang the southern route of the Silk Road reached Khotan lying below the south-western part of the Taklamakan desert, at the foot of the Kun Lin mountain. It had a reputation for silk, rugs and jade, the latter according to Confucius exemplifying not only the perfect man but also carrying the promise of immortality. One particular fable in Buddhism relates the story called 'The King of Rats' in which rats helped the people of Khotan, whose town was being invaded, by gnawing through the harness and bowstrings of the enemy Huns. Many centuries later the great traveller Sir Aurel Stein visited the site and found the tale had changed. The King of Khotan had become a Muslim saint slain in the battle against the Buddhists, the rats becoming transformed into traitors from a nearby village who had entered the Muslim camp at night disguised as dogs which had disarmed the enemy. In a further twist of the story two sacred doves were released from a Muslim martyr's breast and this was absorbed into subsequent legend. In Stein's day thousands of pigeons flew above the shrine of 'my King's castle in the Sand' which now lies at a distance from Khotan in the desert and is called 'The Pigeon Shrine'. It was said that any bird of prey that attacked the pigeons would die as it swooped. On Stein's last visit to the shrine he recorded:

> I made my food offering to the sacred pigeons a duty which my followers would not allow me to neglect. In their eagerness to secure the holy birds' goodwill for the long journey ahead they had carried some Charaks of grain to be brought along.

Further light was thrown on Chinese breeds by the discoveries of Dr. Scully in 1875. In the city of Yarkand, which lies west of Khotan, he found 26 new varieties of pigeon with local names derived from Persian and Chinese sources. Skins of the pigeons were brought back to England and woodcuts were prepared. These show several individual features including a shell-head crest, breast-mottling and the singular beak cresting or nasal tuft whose feathers turn upwards and not downwards which sometimes becomes exaggerated as a frontal tuft.

Four varieties of pigeon reported from Yarkand by Dr. Scully and drawn by J.M. Combe Williams for Poultry magazine in 1885.

The Ak Bash Zagh

The Kara Tokum Damdar

The Char Bash

The Sidam Rakhshi

Due north of Yarkand lies Kashgar where in the past decade Colin Thubron makes passing reference to pigeon soup on the menu of a 'dining room' which he visited and which he described as displaying Chinese influence in the decor.

Progressing north-west from Kashgar, the Silk Road crossed the Chinese border and travelled across Tajikistan towards Sammarakand. In the past, this great city was inhabited by the Sogdians, an ethnic Iranian cult with links to Zoroastrianism, who ruled from 300 BC to 200 AD. They were the greatest merchants of the day who spoke the *lingua franca* of the Silk Road and acted as go-betweens for the traders of East and West. Sammarakand was also an important centre of the Manichean religion founded by the Persian sage Mani in the 3rd century AD. This belief was based on Judaeo-Gnostic, Christian and Persian influences and was also important in introducing Taoism into China. It embodied a great love of nature; its ancient roots, with links to the ancient Mother Goddess, the Babylonian Ishtar with her snakes and temple doves, are reflected in some early traditions and rituals which have been retained until recently. Christian influences include the return of the dove to Noah in the Ark which led to the bird being called 'blessed'. It is also referred to as the soul which returns to the body after death, and is subsequently described as being not only the purest but as being better than any other bird.

Ritual meals were eaten by Manicheans on several feast days which were celebrated on occasions such as the consecration of priests, marriage and death, the latter often being referred to as 'Eating for the Dead'. A surprisingly recent account of such a ceremony was described in 1937 by E.S. Drower in his publication, *The Mandaeans of Iraq and Iran*, in which he witnessed such a ritual. This started with the consecration of a priest; it took place in the cult hut which lay within the sacred enclosure. The dove, which had to be male, perfect and specially bred for the purpose, was slaughtered by the priest in silence. A special knife was used which, together with the dove, was dipped into a sacred pool. The wound of the bird's corpse was then passed through the flame of burning seeds before the breast was removed. The remains of the corpse were then buried beside the cult hut. At the feast, the cakes or biscuits made from specially prepared dough were spread with offerings which included the shredded dove's flesh together with pomegranate seeds, quince, walnuts, coconut and sultan raisins.

The Silk Road eventually reached the northern border of Afghanistan. Below the Hindu Kush mountains lies Mazar-i-Sharif where the beautiful Blue Mosque which was built on the site of the tomb of the prophet Ali-bin-Talib is customarily thronged with white pigeons which are believed to be offerings or blessings to him. Further along the Silk Road close to the border with Iran lies Herat where several decorated dovecote towers were recorded in the 17th century. Further south in Iran itself were the remarkable dovecotes of Isfahan which were built originally to provide manure for the cultivation of melons described as being 'a fruit indispensable to the natives during the great heat of summer'.

Two of the white pigeons at Mazar-i-Sharif being fed from the hand.

Leaving Herat the Silk Road crossed the northern borders of Iran, Iraq and Syria before arriving finally on the Mediterranean coast. At the inland city of Aleppo, south of this point, a link with the pigeon in its role as messenger is to be found. As early as the 12th-14th centuries these birds were extensively used as a pigeon postal service between the cities of Aleppo, Damascus, Baghdad and Alexandria. Later in the 17th century there was a British factory at Aleppo involved in the silk industry. It used the natural harbour at the port of Scandaroon (modern Iskenderun) on the Mediterranean coast of Turkey, whence pigeons conveyed news back of the arrival and departure of ships. It is said that the journey took two and a half hours. The birds, which were housed in their home lofts of Aleppo, were descendants of the original Baghdad homing stock and adopted the name of Scandaroon from the port. An 18th-century record of the history of the town gives details of preparing the bird for flight. A slip of paper with the message was secured under the bird's wing and mention is made that:

> *the feet were bathed in vinegar with a view to keeping it cool and to prevent it being tempted by the sight of water to alight by which the journey might have been prolonged or the billet lost.*

An 18th-century artistic impression of an early pigeon messenger service.

Further Reading

Drower, E.S. (1937), *The Mandaeans of Iraq and Iran*, The Clarendon Press, Oxford

Eliade, M., ed., (1987), *The Encyclopaedia of Religion*, Macmillan, London

Foltz, R.C. (1999), *Religions of the Silk Road*, Macmillan, Basingstoke

Hopkirk, P. (1980), *Foreign Devils on the Silk Road: the search for lost treasures*, John Murray, London

Russell, A. (1794), *The Natural History of Aleppo and parts adjacent*, Vol.10, G..G. and J. Robinson, London

Stein, A. (1903), *Sand-buried Ruins of Khotan*, T. Fisher Unwin, London

Stein, A. (1912), *Ruins of Desert Cathay*, Vols.I & II, Macmillan, London

Thubron, C. (2006), *Shadow of the Silk Road*, Chatto & Windus, London

Whitfield, R. (1990), *Caves of the Thousand Buddhas*, ed. A. Farrer, British Museum Publications, London

Whitfield, S. (1999), *Life along the Silk Road*, John Murray, London

Yanmei, Zhang (2008), *Dunhuang Mogao Grottos*, trans. Han Lei, Better Link Press, New York

The Pigeon as Messenger

Among the pigeon's special attributes its use as a messenger must count as the most outstanding. In particular, its record during both World Wars is a moving and little-known epic. Various references relate the many feats of bravery and endurance which were performed by the birds.

The role of the pigeon as messenger must have been recognised in earliest times. Noah was familiar with it when he released the dove from the ark at the end of the Deluge while a record dating from about 2500 BC in Sumeria, tells of two pigeons being used to carry news of a victory over a trespassing neighbour. Late in the 5th century BC it is believed that Cyrus the Great, founder of the Persian Empire, established a network of pigeon messengers in Assyria which much later in Baghdad was linked with Egypt and the Eastern Mediterranean.

Noah releasing the dove from the Ark. (Fred Aris, Portal Gallery)

The dove of peace with an olive branch.

In Egypt itself pigeons were depicted being released during the coronation procession of Rameses II in 1260 BC and there are references to their use in predicting the progress of the annual flood waters of the Nile. In Greece, in the 6th century BC, a poem refers to the dove carrying a love letter. In a different context Roman ladies were said to have had the habit of taking tame pigeons to the amphitheatre where 'they let them loose from their bosoms' during the spectacle to fly home with a message. There is also a long tradition of messenger pigeons being used in the Arab world to accompany camel caravans across the African Continent while in the Far East in 772-676 BC birds were used by Indian and Arab merchants either by sea or land on visits to China. In China itself their use in carrying news between cities as well as receiving it from incoming junks dates from early times.

During wartime the pigeon's record as messenger is a tale of great heroism. They were used in Roman times, including at the siege of Modena, and during the Crusades in the 12th and 13th centuries. In India in the 16th century Akbar, the Mughal emperor, took the birds on his travels, transported in small cotes (*shown below*).

(right) Early pigeon mail in the Near East. Note the cage holding birds, bottom left.

82

In the Near East the wartime custom is vividly described by the 14th-century English traveller Sir John Mandeville:

> *The people of these countries have a strange custom in time of war and siege; when they dare not send out messengers with letters to ask for help, they write their letters and tie them to the neck of a colver [pigeon] and let the bird fly away. They immediately seek the place where they have been brought up and nourished and are at once relieved of their messages by their owners and desired aid is sent to the besieged.*

Two 15th-century woodcuts, showing pigeons carrying messages tied round their necks.

In Europe it was not until the 19th century that a pigeon post had become established. The birds were quicker than the mail-coaches and provided a well known adjunct to other means of communication. In 1851 when the Reuters news agency was founded, pigeons were employed, not only in addition to telegraphy, but also to fill missing gaps in the railway networks, particularly between Berlin and Paris. During the siege of Paris in 1870-77, towards the end of the Franco-Prussian war, homing pigeons were flown out of Paris in 65 balloons, two of which were lost. The birds were then established in lofts outside the battle zone from which military dispatches and other

PIGEON POST

CARRYING IMPORTANT MESSAGES HOME

Pigeons being released from a balloon flown from Paris.

correspondence could be relayed both inside and outside France.

At the outbreak of the First World War in the United Kingdom, the authorities, fearing that some of the large numbers of pigeons in domestic lofts might be used for espionage, banned the transit of all birds and at the same time ordered the owners to clip their wings. Many were spared this, however, and breeders gave between 100,000 and 200,000 birds to the war effort. The Naval Pigeon Service was established in 1914 and pigeons were carried by submarines and minesweepers. Royal Air Force planes also carried birds which were to be released in case of forced landings or other emergencies. Land forces were not provided with pigeons until 1916 when the British Carrier Pigeon Service was formed and birds were sent to the battlefields where they were generally housed in mobile lofts.

(above) Model of a horse-drawn pigeon loft used on the Western Front in the First World War.

(right) Motorised pigeon loft used behind the trenches in the First World War. (Royal Signals Museum, Blandford)

Many British tanks were also provided with pigeons that were sometimes the only means of communicating with base. At the same time both French and German armies had active carrier pigeon units. Speaking of the value of homing pigeons, the chief of the Department of Signals and Communication has been quoted as saying:

> It is to the pigeon on which we must depend when every other method fails. During quiet periods we can rely on telephones, telegraph signals, the dogs and various other ways in use on the front with the British Army but when the battle rages and everything gives way to barrage and machine-gun fire, to say nothing of gas attacks and bombing, it is to the pigeon we go for succour. I am glad to say they have never failed us.

During the Second World War improved telecommunications reduced the need for pigeons to some extent but thousands of birds were given by British breeders to the National Pigeon Service at the outbreak of war. They were used in all the services and served not only in Europe but also as far afield as India, Burma and North Africa. The bird also played a hazardous role in both wars in the British Intelligence Service, helping to maintain contact with sympathisers and resistance movements in occupied territory. More than 16,000 birds were sent across the channel but it has been estimated that fewer than 10% returned. In practice, batches of pigeons, each wearing its own canvas body harness containing grain and a message

World War I badge from a pigeon unit, with lugs for attachment to a beret. (photograph by James Hansell)

asking French civilians for information, were jettisoned singly from a plane. The risks to the birds on landing were very high. If not found, they died of starvation; if discovered by the enemy, their only hope was to be released with a counter-espionage message. Invaluable details about German V1 and V2 rocket sites across the channel were relayed back. Strategic information was also gathered for the Allied landings on D-Day. The birds were carried routinely by the RAF on bomber planes and were particularly useful in sea-rescue emergencies.

A 'pigeon parachute' used in both world wars. (Barbara Frears)

Night-time view of a dinghy carrying survivors of a British plane downed during the Second World War. One of them is releasing a pigeon with a message seeking help. (by courtesy of The RAF Museum, London)

An intriguing combination used by both British, American and German armies, was the joint use of dogs and pigeons, often to locate wounded soldiers and to secure a two-way line of communication. The trained dogs wore special harnesses carrying a pigeon in a container on each side (*shown right*). On reaching their destination the birds were released, sent at different intervals for the sake of safety, with a message giving the location to the point of command.

In the United States a publication of 1886, relating to messenger birds, noted that: 'In our country pigeons are more largely used than is generally known'. This referred to

86

pigeons taking messages in cities between business men; in office and factory; among suburban home dwellers; by farmers using them from the post office to the city; and by country physicians. In the late 19th century an interest in the birds as messengers was proposed for military purposes but when the United States entered the First World War there was no organised scheme. Eventually, however, in 1918 a military pigeon service attached to the Signal Corps trained the birds for the task ahead; on the front in France they operated from mobile lofts. At the outbreak of the Second World War, private breeders gave birds to the United States Pigeon Service which operated on the Pacific front, as well as in Europe, Asia, Africa and elsewhere. A tribute paid by a general while part of the American landing at Anzio in Italy noted that on account of 'mountainous terrain, poor roads and undependable wire communication, the use of pigeons was imperative'.

In Britain, Europe and the United States pigeons' heroism in both world wars has been recognised by individual awards to the birds and occasionally tributes paid to their military units. No doubt, however, large numbers died unknown and unrecorded. It is difficult to single out particular examples among so many. In Britain, the Dickin Medal, which is regarded in the animal world as the equivalent of the Victoria Cross, was awarded to a bird named 'Winkie' in the Second World War. This pigeon, although

A German dove of peace awarded various decorations of war.

wet and bedraggled, flew from an aircraft which had ditched 120 miles out in the North Sea with a message that saved the crew of grateful airmen who later made a trophy in his memory. In the United States other feats of valour were also recognised, 'Cher Ami' being one of many others in the First World War. This bird served in France and saved hundreds of

'Winkie' with his Dickin Medal and trophy. (Barbara Frears)

soldiers during an incident in which they were cut off and surrounded by the enemy. The bird flew through a barrage of shells and bullets, was hit and arrived back wounded with one leg shattered; the men were saved. The pigeon's body has been mounted and placed in the Smithsonian Institution, Washington DC.

Civic memorials also recognise and remind us of the pigeons' valour in both World Wars. In Europe, imposing edifices at Verdun in France, and in Brussels and Berlin, commemorate birds lost in the First World War. Regrettably the British have not matched this example but in the Second World War a modest individual headstone at the animal cemetery of the People's Dispensary for Sick Animals marks the grave of 'Mary of Exeter'. This hen bird flew many missions and was often wounded; at one time she bore 22 stitches in her tiny body. Another small memorial to 'warrior birds' stands in a municipal park in Worthing, Sussex but unfortunately it has been repeatedly vandalised. In the United States an impressive piece of contemporary sculpture named The Peace Fountain must surely count among memorials to the pigeon. It is made of circular tiers of bronze doves representing 50 states and seven continents.

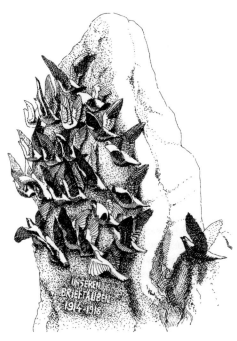

The Berlin Spandau memorial to pigeons lost in the First World War. (Barbara Frears)

The individual headstone erected at the PDSA cemetery to the memory of 'Mary of Exeter'. (Barbara Frears)

The memorial in Brussels to pigeons lost in war. It incorporates a helmet on a pillar surrounded by birds. (Nicholas Philpot)

The Peace Fountain in Rochester, New York.

It was an occasion for great celebration in 2004 when the Animals in War memorial was erected in Park Lane, London. This impressive edifice, carrying the moving epithet 'They had no choice', commemorates all creatures involved in both conflicts. On the main stone façade a procession of the various animals is depicted with three pigeons in flight leading the way.

(right and below) Three doves in flight lead the procession of all creatures involved in both World Wars on the façade of the Animals in War memorial in London.

The Scandaroon

Among the large number of pigeon varieties that have been bred over the centuries, the Scandaroon must count as one of the most unusual. Resembling more a fierce bird of prey than a peaceful granivorous bird, it is a striking looking pigeon with an upright habit, falcon-like appearance and having a pronounced curved beak. An early writer particularly emphasised this feature:

> *the entire head and beak should be of a hooked character, the fact that the longer beak and the more bent and crooked and 'down-faced', the better in the eyes of the present-day experts.*

The Scandaroon, painted by J.W. Ludlow, from Robert Fulton's Illustrated Book of Pigeons, 1895.

The colour of the bird ranges from self-coloured in red, yellow, black & white, as well as pied and silver. Today, a few enthusiasts in the UK and the USA raise the breed as fancy birds while fanciers in Nürnburg, Germany have gained a special reputation in this field.

The Scandaroon belongs to the group known as Wattle pigeons which includes the Baghdad or Eastern Carrier, the renowned messenger bird of the Near East. This latter bird has very ancient origins and was once called the pigeon of Nebuchadnezzar. Centuries later, the English Carrier, known as the king of pigeons, was bred from it; also allied to it is the crooked-beaked bird, the Scandaroon.

The English name Scandaroon was acquired in the 18th century when the bird was used as a messenger to carry information from the Turkish port of that name to an English factory in Aleppo. A widespread tradition had already existed for the use of the birds in this way between the cities of Damascus, Baghdad, Cairo and Alexandria.

The Eastern Carrier from which the Scandaroon originated.

The Scandaroon, drawn by J.C. Lyell in 1886.

Charles Sibillot named this pigeon with the curved beak the Dove of Osiris (*Sibillot's image shown left*). The dove-like bird depicted on the back of the sacred bull, symbol of the God Apis who was a later form of Osiris and also God of the Nile in inundation, is one of the few images linked with the bird in this connection (*shown overleaf*). Also supporting this supposition is the fact that Horus, the son of Osiris and known as the falcon god, was often depicted with the head of a hawk, which hawk which might readily have been confused with the head of a Scandaroon or Baghdad.

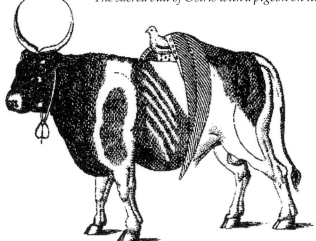

The sacred bull of Osiris with a pigeon on its back. (Barbara Frears)

In classical times, the use of pigeons as messengers was well-known and they are alluded to in myths and legends as early as the 6th century BC. One story relates that during Alexander the Great's expedition to the oracle of Ammon in the Libyan desert, he and his followers having become lost were eventually guided to the Oasis by a flock of pigeons. Sibillot suggests that Alexander, whose tutor was Aristotle, took a great interest in pigeons and their use in divination and for sending messages. On this occasion he ordered that his departure should be signalled by a flight of the birds. Sibillot singles out two Greek coins of the period to support this idea (*shown right*). One shows Alexander holding a pigeon on his out-stretched hand while in the other an upright bird having a markedly hooked beak of the Scandaroon type is shown.

There was a long tradition in the early Arab Middle East of using carrier pigeons, probably of the Baghdad or Scandaroon type; they were sometimes known as King's angels. In 775 AD in Baghdad the service of the 'pigeon-mail' was promoted and encouraged in the caravans of the desert and for sending birds from ships with messages. In 1146 the sultan Nur ed-Din, whose rule reached as far as Syria, Egypt and Sudan, established a system for sending not only official messages but occasionally personal ones as well. A recently discovered document tells of an amorous Caliph who sent his 'favourite' 2,000 little sweets tied to the necks of many pigeons. The methods of attachment to the birds varied and included being tied to the wing, tail, leg or around the neck: special lightweight paper was used similar to that of the miniature portable versions of the *Koran* (*Qur'an*) sometimes carried by Muslims as protective amulets.

There are oblique references to the use of carrier birds in the prosperous and elegant culture of Moorish Spain in the 11th and 12th centuries. It is reasonable to suppose that, at that time, carrier birds such as Baghdads and Scandaroons would have been introduced for the purpose from the Near East. It was a period when Jews, Christians and Muslims lived in tolerance, side by side.

The Muslims had already established their reputation for writing poetry, an example of which, *The Ring of the Dove*, was written in the 11th century by Ibn Hazm of Cordoba, as referred to earlier. It illustrates their literary accomplishment but the jaunty style of the verses in which the lover explains his choice of the bird may owe more to the 20th-century translator than to the original poet.

Old Noah chose a dove to be
His faithful messenger and he
Was not confounded so to choose
She brought him back the best of news.

So I am trusting to this dove
My messages to thee, my love,
And so I send her forth, to bring
My letters safely in her wing.